The

TERROR
—*of the*—
LORD

The

TERROR
—— *of the* ——
LORD

Expanding our understanding of the character of GOD

Mark E. Sheldon

Carpenter's Son Publishing

The Terror of the Lord

Published by Carpenter's Son Publishing, Franklin, Tennessee
Published in association with Larry Carpenter of Christian Book Services, LLC

www.christianbookservices.com

Scripture quotations are taken from the King James Version of the Bible.

Edited by Bob Irvin

Cover Design by 99 Designs
Interior Design by Adept Content Solutions
Printed in the United States of America
ISBN: 978-1-946889-87-4

Knowing therefore
The terror of the lord,
We persuade men.

(2 Corinthians 5:11)

CONTENTS

Introduction

Through the ages, trying to describe the character of God has always been a tremendous challenge to Christians. If any one person were to spend an entire lifetime making a loving and conscientious effort to do so, we could agree that this would be a most worthy effort. As Christians, we are to spend our lives growing in the knowledge and grace of our Lord. However, because God is infinite, we will never be able to exhaust the unfathomable depths of His character. Indeed, that makes the search to better know God more interesting and challenging. Once we know Him, it is our duty to introduce the Lord to a lost and dying world. Given His inexhaustible greatness, the conveying of His character becomes a monumental task.

When we begin to share God's personality and character with others, we have the immense responsibility of describing to them His entire being. We must be careful to balance the characteristics of the Lord's mercy with His judgment, God's grace with His holiness, and His longsuffering with His anger.

Christianity has done an excellent job of showing the more "desirable" attributes of God—if, indeed, it can be put that way (for all His attributes are to be desired). But we have neglected to balance the teaching of God's love with the equally important truth that He will judge each person who has ever lived. However, the pendulum of emphasis has swung to the side of His love and mercy for a long time. And it must be stated here, again, that we could never exhaust teaching the wonders of His love in a thousand lifetimes.

But the pendulum needs to swing back. Not all the way to a judgmental and legalistic God, but to a balanced expression of His personality. There needs to be a declaration of His *terror* by those who know Him to those who know Him not. We who know Him are neglecting to warn people of the consequences of taking God too lightly.

And taking Him lightly is precisely what we are doing. Unbelievers have always had a reckless attitude toward God. That is no surprise. But Christians today are doing the same. We are living in an era of self-serving motivations. Even in Christian society, we don't want to lay ourselves down for the good of others. The idea of self-denial has become virtually obsolete. Anything that God would truly have us do we see as an annoying inconvenience. We shun God's ordained opportunities to be included in His marvelous work of saving lost people from an eternal hell.

Whole congregations attend church Sunday after Sunday without ever hearing words like *sin, judgment,* and *hell.* Ministers and leaders teach year after year, never touching on phrases like "the anger of the Lord" and "the fear of the Lord." We teach too lightly, preach too lightly, pray too lightly, and the result is *the world takes God too lightly.*

Even the secular world is noticing this lack of fervor by the church.

The Tennessean newspaper ran a troubling headline on an Easter Sunday morning, way back in 1992. It read: "Hell's Not a Hot Topic Right Now." Rest assured, Hell is as hot as it has ever been. It's the preaching that has cooled. If preachers won't preach about Hell, who will? If the churches won't warn sinners about Hell, who will?

One of the greatest sermons ever preached was titled "Sinners in the Hands of an Angry God," and was delivered by Jonathan Edwards. It was reported that Edwards only read the sermon. He did not use power points or theatrics and delivered little in the way of hand gestures. The power of conviction was so intense that women sometimes fainted, and grown men would hold onto their pews for fear of the reality of the Hell that was being preached.

This one message was used by God to start a revival that swept this nation. Edwards began his sermon with the verse from Deuteronomy 32:35: "Their foot shall slide in due time . . . " (*King James Version*, as are all Bible uses in this book.) By the way, when is the last time you even heard that verse? For that matter, when is the last time you heard a sermon from the book of Deuteronomy? More important: where are these sermons today? Where are these preachers today? As Ravenhill so profoundly stated in his book, *Why Revival Tarries*: "We have too many dead men in the pulpits giving out too many dead sermons to too many dead people."

Edwards quoted this passage in Deuteronomy to make a distressing point: that sinners were *always exposed to destruction*, just as one who stands or walks in slippery places is exposed to falling. To back the Scripture up further, Edwards referenced Psalm 73:18: "Surely thou didst set them in slippery places; thou castedst them down into destruction."

Paul wrote: "Knowing, therefore, the terror of the Lord, we persuade men" (2 Corinthians 5:12). He did not say, "Knowing, therefore, the 'love' of the Lord." And Jonathan Edwards did not call his message, "Sinners in the Hands of a *Loving* God." Yes, God is love. Yes, Paul wrote that great love chapter in 1 Corinthians chapter thirteen. But just as much as God loves the sinner, He also *hates sin*. We must tell the whole story!

Regrettably, we are not! And the reason that we are not is simple.

Sin. It is our sin. We are not studying to show ourselves approved unto God. We are allowing pastors and preachers to go unchallenged as they pass along their version of the gospel. In many cases, it is a warped picture. It is a shaded and shadowed picture. It lacks the depth and dimension and the description of His fullness. And we do not recognize that their pastel presentation of Him differs dramatically from the biblical unveiling of His wonder. The fault lies with us. We may feel we are doing some good works as a church, but we have left our first love. We are spending our time at a thousand things other than in real, one-on-one fellowship with, and devotion to, our Almighty Creator. In far too many instances we have let *good* become the enemy of *best*.

This book is not an attempt to create a new gospel. It is not a call to some old form of legalism. Neither the world nor Christians need that. What is needed is a new expression of the strength and authority of the old gospel. This will not happen without a considerable change in our understanding of God.

There is a war going on. Satan is leading the charge against us. We have an enemy who wants us spiritually dead and physically dead. We are in this war whether we want to be or not. No amount of effort to avoid participation in this war will make any difference. All attempts to stay on the sidelines will not keep this enemy from trying to destroy us and our loved ones. We must fight! We must fight for our relationship with our heavenly Father, and we must fight for the very souls of all those close to us.

This can only be accomplished with a serious look inward and a renewed look upward. We must recapture the understanding of God's plan for eternity. Not just for us but for those who do not trust in the salvation offered through His Son. For us, the blessings of Heaven will be beautiful beyond description, but for those not trusting in God's offer, the terrors of hell will be eternally horrific.

Because of the unnerving nature of this approach, we will discuss the security of the believer. Not to dispel this magnificent doctrine of hope, but to enlighten us on the unequivocal assurance of salvation that we have in Christ Jesus.

This will be a sobering look. But, at the same time, it will be a rewarding look. After all, we will look into the very face of God and feel the pounding of His heart. It is a heart that beats with His love. It is a face that searches to and fro upon the whole earth looking for those who would love Him.

We will look at a side of God's character that is often overlooked. That side of Himself that has the absolute right to send a sinful man to an awful hell. It will be an unsettling look—but a needful one. We will examine the Scriptures regarding His anger and His wrath. We will see how serious-minded God is about what the future holds for everyone, Christian and sinner alike. Hopefully, the profound impact of urgency will grip our souls.

He is a God whose perfection will not be compromised. He is a God whose grace will bring us to that perfection as He conforms us to the image of His dear Son.

> *For the eyes of the Lord run to and fro throughout the whole earth, to shew himself strong in the behalf of them whose heart is perfect toward him (2 Chronicles 16:9).*

Chapter One

The Warning

*Nevertheless, if thou **warn the wicked** of his way to turn from it; if he do not turn from his way, he shall die in his iniquity; but thou hast delivered thy soul (Ezekiel 33:9).*

One night in the summer of 1966, little did I know that a lesson I was about to learn would have a profound effect on my life. It would be a spiritual lesson. It would have eternal ramifications. And I wasn't even a Christian.

I had graduated from high school earlier that year. It was late in the evening, and I was returning home from a date. Suddenly, a lone set of headlights appeared over the hill. Those lights were coming toward my car, swerving from one side of the road to the other. The car seemed out of control and was approaching at a high rate of speed.

I wondered if the driver would get his car under control. The car drew closer. It was upon me. I veered to the right, sliding to a stop on the shoulder. The out-of-control vehicle made one last swerve and then flipped. In my rearview mirror, I could see the car begin to roll past me, side over side—once, twice, three times. It skidded off the road on its top, slamming into a telephone pole and coming to rest upside down.

Needless to say, it was terrifying to witness.

Leaping from my car, I ran to see if I could help. Just as I crossed the lonely stretch of highway, the engine of the wrecked vehicle burst into flames. I raced to the car to see if anyone was still inside. There were two teen boys hanging upside down from their seatbelts. The driver was conscious, but the passenger was not. As I lay on my stomach, trying to free the driver, he was already going into shock. He kept repeating, quietly, "Please help me. Somebody, please help me."

I managed to loosen his belt and pull him through the broken side window. By now, the flames of the burning engine were growing stronger, shooting higher. Time was running short, and it didn't appear I could free the other boy. No other cars had passed by yet. Observing the light of a nearby house, I sprinted to the door and knocked. A woman who lived there was quick to fill a bucket with water and, returning to the car, I was relieved to see a policeman had arrived and was extinguishing the fire.

The officer turned to me and said he needed my help. It seemed this car had broken the pole, snapping a very high voltage line. It was dark, and neither of us could see where the line was laying. He handed me some flares and said, "Move up the road a little and warn those that come by of the danger. The lines are hanging from the trees and could fall from the branches at any time."

You might expect that the lesson I learned that night had to do with teenagers and drinking too much or driving too fast. These are useful lessons to learn, but it was not at all what God had prepared to show me.

Running to the top of the hill, I struck a flare and began waving it at an oncoming car. It came to a stop, and the folks inside rolled down the window as I explained the danger ahead and suggested they turn around and take a different route. They thanked me for the warning and did just that.

You would think the response of everyone that night would have been one of gratitude for the warning. But instead, this was the lesson I would learn: *Not everyone listens to warnings*. The next car's driver reacted differently. He did not stop, but only slowed and, cracking a window, nodded as those in the car passed by, barely listening to my report of danger ahead. The driver continued, not turning around, believing he could maneuver through the threat on his own. I was baffled by the response but had little time to dwell on it because a third car was approaching.

This response would turn out to be the most bewildering. The vehicle barely slowed. Ignoring the flares and flashing lights of the police car, these people proceeded on with seemingly no concern for the dangers that lay ahead.

Someone has well said that there are three groups of people: those who have sought God and found Him, those who have sought God but not found Him, and those that have not sought God nor found Him.

The lesson I learned that summer night in 1966 concerned a similar three groups.

THE FIRST CAR

The first car I warned was like the first group—those who have sought and found God. They believe the clear warnings of the Scriptures. In its purest form, the Bible's message is: Repent and be saved. In hearing about our lost condition and the results that follow if we are not saved, we repent; we turn away from the dangers of a lost eternity and the horrors of an everlasting hell. We listen to those who have been set as watchmen on the wall telling us of the *terror of the Lord* that awaits those who willfully ignore the warnings. We acknowledge the truth of Heaven if we do repent and hell if we do not. We gratefully accept the instruction of Scripture to turn away from the things that are a danger to our soul, and we are content to let God be the authority on all things good or evil.

Paul knew all about the love of God and was prompted to list what is and is not love in chapter thirteen of First Corinthians. But let us not forget he wrote a second letter to that church in which he said one of the primary motivating factors working in him to persuade men to accept the God of the Bible was the terror of the Lord. The Spirit of God was cautious and precise in His choosing the word *terror*. In the Greek, that word is *phobos*, from which we get our English word phobias. Some of the most common phobias are fears of snakes, spiders, closed-in spaces, heights, and more. Call up your deepest, darkest fear and remember how profoundly it affects your emotions and you begin to get a feeling of how horrible *the terror of the Lord* can be.

The word *terror* does not mean simply, or only, a healthy reverence. It means . . . terror! All we must do to get some understanding of the depth of that terror is to look at Jesus' suffering on the cross. All that Jesus suffered—every stripe, every nail, every hair pulled from his beard, every thorn pushed into his brow—was God's wrath being poured out against sin.

The driver of the first car gave the right response. He stopped at the sign of the signal flare. He and any passengers listened to the warning of what lay ahead. They were persuaded of the seriousness of the danger, and they heeded the recommendation to turn around and go another way.

The Second Car

The second car was like the group that seeks God but does not find Him. The people in that car heard the caution but believed they were all right. They thought they could go on without heeding the caution. They slowed a little, but still chose to ignore what they had been told. What can be said to someone like this to get them to reconsider the consequences of rejecting the warning? Paul was saying, "I tried to tell you of God's love, but you didn't get it, so let me tell you about His anger." In the book of Jude, it says: "of some have compassion, making a difference: and of others *save with fear*, pulling them out of the fire" (vv. 22, 23).

It seems quite clear that some folks do not respond to the message of love but do respond to a sermon on fear. Don't think for a moment that God wants anyone to go to hell. "For this is good and acceptable in the sight of God our Saviour; Who will have all men to be saved, and to come unto the knowledge of the truth" (1 Timothy 2:3, 4). But a lost sinner can only be pulled from the fires of hell while here on earth. The book of Hebrews tells us this: *It is appointed unto man once to die and then the judgment.*

DECEIVED

Many lost people, if they give eternity a thought, believe God will have mercy on everyone in the end. But a simple question must be asked: then what was the purpose of the cross? How cruel to make Jesus go through all His suffering if everyone enters Heaven in the end. God will not use a cosmic eraser at the end of one's life. It makes no difference how good we think we are. It matters not if we think we are a little better than others. What matters is what God says, and we are entirely guilty as far as the Lord is concerned. "For whosoever shall keep the whole law, and yet offend in one point, *he is guilty of all*" (James 2:10, emphases placed in Scriptures in this book are mine—M.S.). It is not what we do for the Lord that gets us into Heaven. It is what He did for us—and whether we believe we needed it. Our destiny depends on our response.

THE THIRD CAR

The third car was like the third group. The driver of that car never listened, and he certainly did not stop. This group is the most frightening of all. They never seek God and never *want* to seek God—and thus will never find him. This is the group that will experience the full-blown terror and anger of God. These individuals won't be persuaded. Jesus said there would be those who would not believe even if someone came back from the dead. *And he did just that.* He rose from the grave. They don't believe it, and they won't trust it, and only the horrors of hell await them. Be honest. How often do we hear this from the pulpits today?

Jesus often spoke about hell. Our Savior, the greatest preacher to ever live, spoke more about hell than Heaven! It makes you wonder why eternal damnation and the torture it will bring is such an avoided topic in today's churches.

Why do preachers stay away from even mentioning it? Why do people not want to hear it? The answer to the second question is probably more apparent than the answer to the first. It is *uncomfortable.* It makes people squirm. The images are all too real. Imagined pictures of gnashing teeth and burning in fire forever, but never being burned up, are hauntingly vivid. Unfortunately, the congregations—fearing the truths of such an awful eternity—either consciously or subconsciously dictate the limiting or full-blown absence of this part of the gospel. Some are lulled to sleep without the specific confrontation of an eternity apart from God, while others are actively responsible for an "itching ears" mentality.

> For the time will come when they will not endure sound
> doctrine; but after their own lusts shall they heap to
> themselves teachers, having itching ears, And they shall
> turn away their ears from the truth (2 Timothy 4:3, 4).

Paul is telling Timothy the time is coming when people will not listen to solid biblical teaching. No matter how thorough the message covers real Scriptural truth, it is not going to satisfy their desire. And to make matters worse, they will turn away from what they *need* to hear and go searching for teachers who will tell them what they *want* to hear. Paul uses the word *heaping.* In other words, they will find countless false teachers who will feed their self-esteem. It is certainly evident that there are numerous teachers out there just waiting to oblige them.

But what about the preachers? Preachers should not be listening to the people; the people should be listening to the preachers. We should not let the masses tell us what to preach; we should let God tell us what to preach. We should not tell them what they want to hear, we should preach to them what they *need* to hear. What they need to understand is the whole counsel of God. Even if they do not want to listen to it, we are still to preach it.

The gospel is offensive. We cannot change that, nor should we attempt to alter its message. To take the approach of not offending anyone plays directly into the Devil's hands. It works in his favor if the "watchmen" ignore preaching the consequences of sin. It makes his enticements even more alluring. The cry of the lost soul screams, "I can't be all that bad! The terror you are suggesting can't be as bad as all that!" And that mind-set becomes the rationale for all manner of sin.

But the message of *"knowing, therefore, the terror of the Lord, we persuade men"* runs smack dab into the fleshly nature of rebellious humanity. Preaching hell lays down the gauntlet. It says: Now you know the *rest* of the story. Sin if you will, but rest assured that whatsoever you sow, that shall you also reap.

Chapter Two

The Crucifixion

*Him [Jesus], being delivered by the determinate coun-
sel and foreknowledge of God, ye have taken, and by
wicked hands have crucified and slain (Acts 2:23).*

T o see the proof of God's wrath, we need look no further than the cross of Christ. All His anger was on display more than two thousand years ago. The cross was a preordained event that the Father, the Son, and Holy Spirit agreed upon before the foundation of the world. The Lord had made the plan to save us before He set creation in motion. Taking a closer look at the Scriptures on this topic, it is interesting to note that God did this from the point of His wrath.

*For we which have believed do enter into rest, as he
said, As I have sworn **in my wrath** if they shall enter
into my rest: although the works **were finished from
the foundation of the world** (Hebrews 4:3).*

In layman's terms, before the day of creation, the triune God-head decided on all that they would create. At the top of His creation list was man. We would be made in the image of God. The heavenly

Father would give to mankind free will. Free will is the key here. The Lord was *not* predestinating the soul of any man. Where we spend eternity is our choice completely.

Some respond to the call to come to a loving God. Some respond to the call of the fear of the Lord. Both the loving approach and the fire and brimstone approach are ordained by the Lord. Both are to be employed by the church to bring about the same result. The Creator of the universe wants us to repent and call upon the name of the Lord that we might be saved. God, in His infinite wisdom, knew that man would choose to rebel against Him. God's character would rightfully be angered at this choice, and His wrath would be kindled. But His love planned to save us from our disobedient decision. Thus, the plan for Jesus (God in the flesh) to die to pay the debt of our sins was founded. Peter explained it this way: "Who verily was foreordained before the foundation of the world, but was manifest in these last times for you" (1 Peter 1:20). Our eternal destination was not foreordained, but the plan to save us was preplanned. The Bible is clearly saying this: God's wrath would have to be handed out against our rebellion. He could not just ignore His anger nor forget about it and move on; to be entirely just in His holy character He would pour out that wrath. God is Holy, and He must punish sin. By His character, being equal in its mercy and wrath, He chose to pour His judgment upon Himself.

God's terror and His love collided the day of His Son's crucifixion. Both His wrath and His mercy were on display in a perfect balance of His nature. It was both the wages of sin and the gift of God hanging in plain view for all to see. Now imagine those who will not believe. Look back at Hebrews 4:3: those who will believe may enter God's rest. But those who won't believe now remain under the same fierce wrath that was put on Jesus. God laid on Jesus all the sins of the world. All those who choose not to believe this are doomed to experience the same severity of punishment that Jesus suffered. The difference is they will suffer for all eternity. It will be a ghastly existence "where their worm dieth not, and the fire is not quenched" (Mark 9:44, 46, 48).

CHOICE

We have a choice in this life as well. It is a choice between heaven and hell. Between the most magnificent eternity ever or the worst eternity ever. The Bible says that we have a decision to make in this life. Joshua 24:15 is clear: "Choose ye this day whom ye will serve . . . As for me and my house, we will serve the Lord." The cross is visible to all. The way to Heaven is easily understood. Jesus said He is the way. He made it transparent to all. No one comes to the Father but by Him. You want Heaven? Choose Jesus!

The problem lies with the fact that worldly gifts are also visible. Satan makes them appear as if they are great. Adultery, lust, greed, lying, cheating, stealing, power, prestige, possessions—all of these and more are out there and look enticing to a world that turns away from the cross. To them, the cross is a trivial gift. That "crucifixion thing" is a distant Easter story with no real significance. A life of self-sacrifice seems horrible. Denying themselves anything goes against all the cries of their flesh.

But someday they will be standing before the Lord having already sealed their fate by the choice they made in this life. It will be moments before their final banishment. They will take one last look at the One who was crucified for their sin. There will be terror in what they see. They will see Jesus face to face. They will see His eyes of fire. They will know that they are before Him for one purpose: to be judged. "His head and his hairs were white like wool, as white as snow; and his eyes were as a flame of fire" (Revelation 1:14).

On the day Jesus was crucified, there were many things that happened. In our theology, we know that He was "made sin"—and that sin was our sin. Death was the penalty being applied that day, in His body, the body that had known no sin. "For he hath made him to be sin for us, who knew no sin; that we might be made the righteousness of God in him" (2 Corinthians 5:21).

Let's take the events of that day apart. Everything that happened to Jesus in those hours was directly related to our sin. The world He came to save had ignored Him for as long as it could—until His very presence in Jerusalem demanded a response. The religious leaders of that day denied Him as the Son of God, and even as he hung dying they denied Him a sip of cool water when He said, "I thirst." It was dusty and dirty, and though He hung bleeding from a tree, they gave him no relief. Their hatred seethed so profoundly within them that they outwardly gritted their teeth. They wanted His destruction and had finally devised a plan for His death. He was as innocent as a baby lamb; they hated Him without a cause. And now their eyes were witnessing the end of this Jesus, and they spoke loudly, seemingly saying: Aha, aha, now we get to watch you die!

> *But in mine adversity they rejoiced, and gathered themselves together: yea, the abjects gathered themselves together against me, and I knew it not; they did tear me, and ceased not:*
>
> *With hypocritical mockers in feasts, they gnashed upon me with their teeth. Lord, how long wilt thou look on? Rescue my soul from their destructions, my darling from the lions. I will give thee thanks in the great congregation: I will praise thee among much people. Let not them that are mine enemies wrongfully rejoice over me: neither let them wink with the eye that hate me without a cause. For they speak not peace: but they devise deceitful matters against them that are quiet in the land. Yea, they opened their mouth wide against me, and said, Aha, aha, our eye hath seen it (Psalm 35:15-21).*

The Bible uses the word *abjects*. It means the hopeless and miserable. You must be incredibly unhappy to hate one so lovely as Jesus Christ the Son of God. To hate Him is to put yourself in the most hopeless condition ever. For without Him there is no hope.

Transferring Punishment

The Bible is clear in teaching us that God transferred all our sin onto His Son at the cross, as we saw in 2 Corinthians 5:21 above.

At the Great White Throne Judgment, the tables will be turned. The wrath that was poured out on Jesus at the cross will now be poured out on everyone who rejected His substitution for them. Imagine the terror people will feel as they are suspended in nothingness before Him. They ignored Christ all their lives, and now He will ignore their pleas for mercy. He had sent the Holy Spirit to garner a response, but they rejected His calling. And now the Lord will reject their calling. They laughed at Him and mocked Him and rejoiced over His suffering. The stark realization of their calamity will bring deep dread to their spirit. They will be facing a panic that borders on hysteria. Their reluctance to know Jesus will find no relief. Their terror will be brought to its highest point at the sudden awareness of their immediate danger. They will be immobilized as they experience fear at its ultimate extreme. They laughed at Him and they mocked Him, but now the situation will be reversed. Jesus will repeat the words of Proverbs 1:26: "I also will laugh at your calamity; I will mock when your fear cometh."

- At the cross, they ignored him. At their judgment He will ignore them. Their cries for mercy will be rejected.

- At the cross, they denied him. At their judgment He will deny them. Matthew 7:23: "And then will I profess unto them, 'I never knew you: depart from me, ye that work iniquity.'"

- At the cross, they wanted his destruction. At their judgment He will pronounce their destruction. Matthew 25:41: "Then shall he also say unto them on the left hand, 'depart from me, ye cursed, into everlasting fire, prepared for the devil and his angels.'"

- At the cross, they hated him. Psalms 25:19: "Consider mine enemies; for they are many, and they hate me with cruel hatred." At their judgment He will show His hatred of their evil. Psalms 26:5: "I have hated the congregation of evildoers, and will not sit with the wicked."

- At the cross, Jesus was innocent. At their judgment He will declare them guilty and will not clear their charge. Exodus 34:7: "Keeping mercy for thousands, forgiving iniquity and transgression and sin, and that will by no means clear the guilty; visiting the iniquity of the fathers upon the children."

- At the cross, they gnashed their teeth at Him. At their judgment He will send them to a hell where they will gnash their teeth forever. Matthew 13:42: "And shall cast them into a furnace of fire: there shall be wailing and gnashing of teeth."

- At the cross, there was three hours of darkness. At their judgment, they will be cast into eternal darkness. Matthew 8:12: "But the children of the kingdom shall be cast out into outer darkness."

This is what Paul had in mind when He penned, *"Knowing, therefore, the terror of the Lord, we persuade men."* No one wants to face such a horror as just described. But so many will. These words have only scratched the surface of the nature of this final confrontation between men who did not pay attention to the value of their souls and the One who was willing to die to save those souls.

WATCHMEN

We are not telling the whole story. Shame on us. We are supposed to be watchmen on the wall. Ezekiel said the blood would be on our hands if we do not warn the lost world. Ezekiel 33:6 says: "But if the watchman sees the sword come, and blow not the trumpet, and the people be not warned; if the sword come, and take any person from among them, he is taken away in his iniquity; but his blood will I require at the watchman's hand."

As watchmen, we see the end coming. The more that God pulls back His hand of protection on this world, the more we see the disastrous effects of sin. From school massacres to rape and murder to war that never ends, man's evil nature becomes more evident. New diseases are born out of licentious lifestyles. Old diseases are making a comeback. The lid is being lifted off political corruption everywhere. Pornographic texting has become epidemic. Drug use is skyrocketing. Add to all this the rash of gruesome crimes, including madmen cannibalizing people in plain view, and the world gasps for a moment . . . only to go back to pretending all is right with the world. All of this is just the surface result of a world turning itself over to unrestrained evil. "What does it profit a man, if he were to gain the whole world and lose his soul?" (Mark 8:36).

Christians know that Jesus indeed is the only way. There is no other plan. We are witnessing what the world would be like without Him. Rest assured, God will not be mocked. He is about to pour out the cup of His anger. "The same shall drink of the wine of the wrath of God, which is poured out without mixture into the cup of his indignation; and he shall be tormented with fire and brimstone in the presence of the holy angels, and in the presence of the Lamb" (Revelation 10:14).

Did you see that, dear reader? His wrath will be poured out *without mixture*! It will not be diluted at all. No compassion will be mixed in nor any mercy be stirred into this cup of wrath. Those who think they will get a second chance after death will be mistaken. Jeremiah 42:18 says, in part, "As mine anger and my fury hath been poured forth upon the inhabitants of Jerusalem; so, shall my fury be poured forth upon you . . . " Look at the word God chooses to define His upcoming judgment on sinners. *Fury!* In other words, His judgment will be intense and furious. The sinner's penalty will be fierce and taken to the extreme. The eternal punishment from God on the sinner will be violent and savage and concentrated wholly on that sinner's rebellion. Some will say that this picture of God is not true. But all you must do to prove these words is to see how violently and savagely Jesus was treated. *Fury, wrath, indignation, fire,* and *brimstone* are words God has chosen to describe His anger. We have been so inundated with the teaching on "God is love" that we fail to understand the balance in His nature. We cannot see—or do not want to see—the truth of all that has been written in the Holy Scriptures concerning His right, as Sovereign of the world, to judge that world.

Add to these thoughts this disturbing verse for those rejecting Christ. Romans 2:5 says: "But after thy hardness and impenitent heart treasurest up unto thyself wrath against the day of wrath and revelation of the righteous judgment of God." Who in their right mind would ever store up wrath to be poured out upon themselves later? I like the King James choice of the word *treasurest*. That word points directly at what a lost heart deems important. (Matthew 6:21: "For where your treasure is, there will your heart be also.") It speaks of an indictment against a stubborn heart, unbending and unresponsive to the warnings of Scripture, all the while stockpiling God's anger and resentment.

MANY WAYS?

Many in this world believe there are many ways to find God. They will ask, "What about the Muslim or the Jew or the Hindu?" The Lord is very clear in his answer. "Jesus saith unto him, I am the way, the truth, and the life: <u>no man cometh unto the Father, but by me</u>"

(John 14:6, emphasis mine). For those who go through any (and all) religious activities apart from the Lord Jesus Christ—these will not be accepted by God the Father. He makes Himself known to everyone. Romans 1:20 states emphatically: "For the invisible things of him from the creation of the world are _clearly seen_, being understood by the things that are made, _even his eternal power and Godhead; so that they are without excuse._" This verse is not complicated. It is unmistakable in its meaning. The world's religions are those that try to blur the meaning. Mankind has one big problem: _sin_. Whether you are Jew or Muslim or Hindu or agnostic or atheist—whoever you are on earth!—there is only one cure for sin. Jesus! God pronounced the penalty for sin: _death_. Romans 6:23: "For the wages of sin is death." God took that penalty upon Himself at the cross. We either believe this and are saved from the penalty of sin, or we don't believe this and the punishment for our sin remains on us. It is no wonder that God gets furious with our dismissal and indifference to the love He expressed for us from that cross. He was under no obligation to save us from our sins.

It seems that much of today's preaching has fallen into a form of "religious correctness." The proclamation of the Gospel is shying away from words like _judgment, repentance, sin,_ and _hell._ The declaration of the Gospel stays in the comfort zone of grace, mercy, and love. Again, let it be stated: these are great truths! Jude says, however, in verses 22, 23 of his book: "And of some have compassion, making a difference: And _others save with fear,_ pulling them out of the fire; hating even the garment spotted by the flesh." God knows that, for whatever reason, there are people unsympathetic to the suffering Jesus experienced on the cross. They have been unresponsive to the gospel approach of grace and mercy. Something needs to shake them up before it is too late. A hard heart needs to be hit hard. Putting a little godly _fear_ back in our sermons would go a long way toward waking these people up.

When we speak of "fire and brimstone" preaching today, it seems to be referring to an old approach used many years ago. The inference is that mankind is now too sophisticated to respond to such an outdated style of conveying the story of Jesus. But it was Jesus Himself who repeatedly used the fire and brimstone analogies in his teachings. Revelation 14:10: "And he shall be tormented with fire and brimstone in the presence of the holy angels and in the presence of the Lamb." He states it again in Luke 12:49: "I am come to send fire on the earth; and what will I if it be already kindled?" By the way, "too sophisticated" is just a substitution for too prideful. God is not spending eternity with prideful people. Isaiah 57:15: "For thus saith the high and lofty One that inhabiteth eternity, whose name is Holy; 'I dwell in the high and holy place, *with him also that is of a contrite and humble spirit*, to revive the spirit of the humble, and to revive the heart of the contrite ones.'"

When was the last time someone reminded you that you can make God very angry? Psalms 2:12: "Kiss the Son, lest he be angry, and ye perish from the way, when his wrath is kindled but a little. Blessed are all they that put their trust in him." This is one of the clearest Old Testament passages speaking about Jesus. He is the Son. The scriptures are exhorting us to "kiss" the Son. In other words, we should express real affection for the One who first loved us. Our affection should be shown outwardly and honestly. It should be demonstrated before He gets angry. We know there is a future time when this anger will be displayed. But it is evident from the Word of God that His anger can be stirred now. Psalms 7:11: "God judgeth the righteous, and *God is angry with the wicked every day.*"

Someone has well said: "The only hell a Christian will experience is here on earth, and the only heaven a lost person will experience is here on earth." We all have this lifetime that God has given us to either believe in His Son or not. The obvious problem is that none of us know how much time we have. Jonathon Edwards quoted from Deuteronomy 32:35 that "their foot shall slide *in due time.*" He drew from those words that God was hanging onto the one on the slippery slope, and it was God's good pleasure to decide when to let go of the sinner's hand. I would never try to guess how the Lord chooses when it is time to end a life. But it must have to do with the Father's remembrance of what His Son went through on that cross.

Jesus took our place of God's judgment when He went to the cross. He was the substitute sinner for anyone who would believe in Him and what He did for them on the cross. He took the sinner's place, and *God did not spare him*. For all who will not believe in Christ, God will not spare them! Jesus cried from the cross: "My God, my God, why hast thou has forsaken me?" (Mark 15:34). It was the worst cry for help the world has ever heard.

Poor sinner, please listen. Without belief in Jesus Christ before you die, your cries will be answered with the words of God from Proverbs 1:25-27: "But ye have set at nought all my counsel, and would none of my reproof: I also will laugh at your calamity; I will mock when your fear cometh; When your fear cometh as desolation and your destruction cometh as a whirlwind; when distress and anguish cometh upon you."

CHAPTER THREE

—— SATAN'S DEVICES ——

Lest Satan should get an advantage of us: for we are not ignorant of his devices (2 Corinthians 2:11).

S atan is our enemy. It matters not whether you are lost or saved. He despises the Christian and non-Christian alike. He hates everything that God loves. He was God's first enemy. When God said that He would make man in His image, Satan's blood was brought to a boiling point. It did not take him long to go after the first man and woman. There he was in the garden, the serpent, ready to deceive. Some theologians believe he appeared within the first week after Adam and Eve's creation. Whatever the time frame, he did not wait long to work to destroy what God had deemed good. "Be sober, be vigilant; because your adversary the devil, as a roaring lion, walketh about, seeking whom he may devour" (1 Peter 5:8). When Jesus entered His public ministry, He went to John the Baptist to be baptized. When He came out of the water, He was immediately led by the Spirit of God into the wilderness. Forty days later, the devil was there to try to derail the Son of God. He attacked Jesus at His weakest.

We know from Scripture that Satan was unsuccessful. He tried the same methods he had employed in the garden of Eden. These are the same strategies he uses today. The Bible says these schemes should not catch us off guard.

Satan has a planned program of attack. The Bible calls it "his wiles" (a trick intended to ensnare or deceive). God commands us to be prepared when the devil assaults us with his tactics. "Put on the whole armour of God, that ye may be able to stand against the wiles of the devil" (Ephesians 6:11). Tempting us to ignore God is the same crafty ploy he has used since the day of his first rebellion. He follows the same game plan every time he tries to lead you and me astray. His system is subtle. He designs ways to lead the believer away from the will of God. He maneuvers the unbeliever from ever knowing the will of God. The devil has no more care for the sinner than the saint. Satanists that think they are getting respect from this evil angel have fallen prey to this great deceiver. Satan only uses them for his self-interests. Once he has exhausted his use of their life he destroys them with the same repugnant disdain he has for Christians. For evidence, just look at all the musicians and Hollywood entertainers who have come and gone, many dying at a premature age. The Devil didn't care, and he doesn't care. In fact, he could not care less.

All lives have meaning in this world. No matter how big or small, whether for good or evil, we all cast an influence on others. There were two men who lived their lives in the same generation. Both were born into Christian homes. Both were in their nineties when they died. They passed away within a year of each other. They both had a profound impact on mankind. One man was Billy Graham. The other: Hugh Hefner. One led men toward Heaven. The other steered men toward hell. One taught men to love God. The other tempted men to love flesh. Satan hated them both. Jesus died for them both. Only one of them believed it.

STRATEGIES

So, what are his strategies? What is his game plan? If we are to fight against it, we need to know. If we are to expose it (and we indeed are), we need to recognize its design. Paul wrote to the Corinthian church that we are to try and persuade men because we understand the terror of the Lord. Satan certainly uses all his tactics to persuade men that there is no such thing as the terror of the Lord. He tempts men, instead, to fear that they are missing out on all the "good times" to be had in this world. But the Bible says, "The fear of the Lord is the beginning of wisdom" (Psalms 111:10). Jesus put it this way: "And fear not them which kill the body, but are not able to kill the soul: but rather fear him which is able to destroy both soul and body in hell" (Matthew 10:28). Talk about the terror of the Lord! If we would seriously consider the destruction that lies ahead for choosing the world, we would be less inclined to fall into the devil's traps. Satan is doing all he can to keep the lost world focused on his enticements. When the Devil is successful, the unbelieving sinner never considers the judgment to come. That leads us to the inroads that Satan has made into the church. The Bible says in 1 Peter 4:17: "For the time comes *that judgment must begin at the house of God*: and if it first begins at us, what shall the end be of them that obey not the gospel of God?" Did you see that? Do you hear that? Judgment must begin with the church, and the church must be preaching judgment. Peter asks a great question at the end of this verse. *What shall the end be of them that obey not the gospel of God?* Knowing the terror of the Lord, the church is supposed to tell the lost what the end will be for them.

BARELY SAVED

We are barely saved ourselves. The righteousness that we have has been given to us by God. We have no righteousness of ourselves. We are only righteous because He made us the righteousness of God in Christ Jesus. Listen again to Peter in his very next verse. 1 Peter 4:18: "And if the righteous *scarcely be saved*, where shall the ungodly and the sinner appear?" The church should be telling the unrighteous where they are going to appear. They are going to appear before Jesus and then be sentenced to hell. If that isn't bad enough, hell will then be cast into the lake of fire. Revelation 20:14: "And death and hell were cast into the lake of fire. This is the second death." Some recoil at this message. They say: "There you go again with that fire and brimstone preaching." Well, let me point out again that this is New Testament. In fact, this is at the end of the New Testament. Revelation 21:8: "But the fearful, and unbelieving, and the abominable, and murderers, and whoremongers, and sorcerers, and idolaters, and all liars shall have their part in the lake which burneth *with fire and brimstone*: which is the second death."

As you might expect, if God is going to start His judgment in the church, then Satan will begin in the church to stop the judgment. You may ask why. The answer is: Because once God has dealt with His children, then He will begin the judgment of Satan and his children. The beginning of the end of evil will be at hand. So Satan fights. He fights like a lion caught in a snare.

No Christian wants anyone to go to hell. God wants no one to perish. Listen to 2 Peter 3:9: "The Lord is not slack concerning his promise, as some men count slackness; but is longsuffering to us-ward, not willing that any should perish, but that all should come to repentance." God wants *all* to repent, but not all will repent. 2 Peter 2:9, 12: "The Lord knoweth how to deliver the godly out of temptations, and to reserve the unjust unto the day of judgment to be punished . . . these, as natural brute beasts, made to be taken and destroyed . . . .and shall utterly perish in their own corruption." Peter made it clear that God will not lead us into temptation. Jesus even taught us to pray, "lead us not into temptation, but deliver us from evil." Many who are lost willingly fall into temptation. Peter uses words seldom heard from pulpits today, words like *judgment, punished, destroyed, perish,* and *corruption*.

Satan has convinced the church to stop talking about hell. There are very few sermons on this topic anymore. Churches are springing up everywhere started by pastors who openly declare that they are not going to mention the old, antiquated topics of judgment, hell, and repentance. Some pastors have gone so far as to canvas communities, asking what the people dislike about church. They continue the questionnaire with: "What don't you want to hear?" And: "What do you want to hear?" With that information in hand, the pastors begin to build a church on the likes and dislikes of lost people. The lost person says: "I do not want sermons on hell. I do not like being told I am a sinner. I want good, positive messages that make me feel better about myself." So instead of bringing the message of God, the pastors preach the message of lost people. Matthew 15:9: "But in vain they do worship me, teaching for doctrines the commandments of men." The preachers just parrot back what the congregation wants to hear. These false teachers are leading the masses and betraying their calling. Deceiving and being deceived, they preach what Satan wants to be preached. 2 Timothy 3:13: "But evil men and seducers shall wax worse and worse, deceiving, and being deceived." This did not catch God off guard. Two thousand years ago, Paul penned a letter to Timothy. 1 Timothy 4:1: "Now the Spirit speaketh expressly, that in the latter times some shall depart from the faith, giving heed to seducing spirits, and doctrines of devils."

The message of the cross offends people. Some do not respond well to hearing that their hearts are incredibly wicked. Their comeback is: "I'm not all that bad." Listen again to the Bible. Jeremiah 17:9: "The heart is deceitful above all things, and *desperately wicked*: who can know it?" As God sees it, there is not much good in our hearts. Again, Genesis 6:5: "And God *saw* that the wickedness of man was great in the earth and that every imagination of the *thoughts of his heart was only evil continually.*"

Satan calls into question the very Word of God. His approach to Eve was, "hath God said?" In other words: did God mean that when He said that? The devil gives his interpretation of the Word of God. He deceived Eve into thinking there would be no penalty. In fact, he deceived her into believing she would get much pleasure and blessing from his "version" of God's word. After all, the fruit would taste good, and she would be like God. She should have told the serpent: "I have an entire garden of great tasting food. And by the way, I am already made in the image of God."

The gospel message needs to be clear again. We need to establish anew that there is a heaven to gain and a hell to pay. Sinners must be told to repent and be saved. This needs to come from the pulpits everywhere. The whole gospel needs to be thundered loudly. We should shout all the words that God has asked us to preach. Listen to Jeremiah (26:2): "Thus saith the Lord: 'Stand in the court of the Lord's house, and speak unto all the cities of Judah, which come to worship in the Lord's house, *all the words that I command thee to speak unto them; diminish not a word.*'" Do not miss the emphasis! Preach all the words! Don't leave any of them out. Why? So that, first, sinners might turn from their evil ways. And second, that God will turn from His readiness to bring wrath. Jeremiah 26:3: "If so be they will hearken, and turn every man from his evil way, *that I may repent me of the evil, which I purpose to do unto them because of the evil of their doings.*"

I can hear the preachers now: "If I start preaching that, my congregation will crucify me." Well, pay heed to how they responded to Jeremiah (26:8): "Now it came to pass when Jeremiah had made an end of speaking all that the Lord had commanded him to speak unto all the people, that the priests and the prophets and all the people took him, saying, Thou shalt surely die." Jeremiah preached it anyway!

The real question is, who do you love? If we love the Lord, we will preach what He has said to preach. Many will be offended. But what about the precious few who hear and obey? Do we love them? Do we love them enough to tell them the whole truth? There are always some who will believe the report. There are always some who will be persuaded by the truth of what has been said. If we are true to the Word of God, the Word of God will be true to those who hearken to it. Let us stop decreasing the severity of the consequences. Those who reject God's call to repentance need to hear of the future punishment for their sin. How can we persuade others if we are not convinced ourselves?

Whenever the pulpit "masters" teach only what they want to teach, the Word of God is being diminished. Each time a pastor ignores studying the passages of Scripture he does not like the Word of God is decreased. Anytime a teacher neglects to teach those passages he does not care for the Word of God is devalued. A neutralized message creates a dispassionate Christianity. Our pleas to a lost world fall on deaf ears because we have no real emotion of truth driving us to call men to be saved. If we believe in an awful hell, we certainly don't want men to go there. If we don't believe God gets angry, we will never convince a soul who is dead in trespasses and sins to repent.

FEAR THE LORD

We are to learn to fear the Lord. It is the beginning of wisdom and knowledge of Him. *Terror* seems to be the perfect word, chosen by Paul, to get across the horror that will come to any soul who turns his back on the salvation offered by God through His Son Jesus Christ.

Satan has attempted to water down the harsh reality of hell. His greatest attack has been in silencing sermons on the topic. It is one thing for *him* to contradict God's word. Humanism is one of the apparent offshoots of that tactic. Those in the world pride themselves on being "free thinkers." The Bible says, in John 1:1: "In the beginning was the Word, and the Word was with God, and the Word was God." Everything started with the Word of God. Any thoughts that came after that, from any "free thinker," has to agree or disagree with what the Word said first. Ecclesiastes 1:9: "The thing that hath been, it is that which shall be; and that which is done is that which shall be done: and *there is no new thing under the sun.*"

The world keeps trying to find a way to justify its brand of morality. Those in the world hope to convince themselves that there are no consequences for their actions. The lost push back every time their behavior is called sin. They believe their approach is setting them free. The opposite is true. The lost in this world are binding themselves deeper into bondage. Not all unbelievers who want to justify their actions agree with the actions of others. But they dare not bring an accusation, or it would open their behavior to scrutiny.

Satan mixes up the interpretation of the Word by the use of contradicting commentaries. Denominations try to legitimize what Scriptures call abominations. Sinners become more emboldened because they believe there is some inherent safety in numbers. As long as the pulpits stay quiet on the coming judgment, the strategy seems to be working. But sin is still sin. Hell is still hot. And the lake of fire is still the destination of anyone who thinks otherwise. It is time we begin to restate the truth. There are some who will hear and respond. But the door is closing. We need to persuade those who still have time to believe before it is too late.

AVOIDING SATAN'S TRAPS

The Devil is no one's friend. He sets his snares for all of us. There is no way to list all the devices he uses to try and capture us. Suffice it to say that his wiles are strategies to take us away from God. He hates God. He hates us. Anything and everything he can do to lure us and take us hostage is on his agenda all the time. We must be watchful for the particular temptations he uses against us individually. 1 Peter 5:8: "Be sober, be vigilant; because your adversary the devil, as a roaring lion, walketh about, seeking whom he may devour." Our vigilance starts with our avoiding danger. The dangers of wrongful thoughts, dangers of wrongful activities, and the dangers of wrongful attitudes tempt us. We are to flee our youthful lusts. That means we are to step aside, turn aside, withdraw, and keep clear of every enticement the Devil offers. We are to duck, dodge, and distance ourselves from every fiery dart he throws our way. We should never give up in our fight against sin. We are not to lay off in the battle for righteousness, but we are to ward off anything that hinders us from imitating our Lord Jesus Christ!

God knows that in our battles we have sometimes been wounded and afflicted. Psalms 119:67: "Before I was afflicted I went astray: but now have I kept thy word." The breakdown in our walk with the Lord begins when we neglect our prayer life and fail to study our Bibles as we should. This is one of the traps of the enemy. He tries to interrupt or eliminate our time spent with the Lord. We must guard our devotional life with all diligence. We must come boldly *before* our God before we can stand boldly *for* our God. Hebrews 4:16: "Let us therefore *come boldly* unto the throne of grace, that we may obtain mercy and find grace to help in time of need." We must refuse the Devil's advances and turn down any of his offers. His temptations can seem strong sometimes, but it is only because our flesh is weak. James 4:7, 8: "Submit yourselves therefore to God. Resist the devil, and he will flee from you. Draw nigh to God, and he will draw nigh to you. Cleanse your hands, ye sinners; and purify your hearts, ye double minded."

Trust in the Lord, dear reader. He always provides a way out. Our Lord always has an escape plan. 1 Corinthians 10:13: "There hath no temptation taken you but such as is common to man: but God is faithful, who will not suffer you to be tempted above that ye are able; but will with the temptation also make *a way to escape*, that ye may be able to bear it." The Devil is a snake, and there is no shame in using God's side door to sidestep that old sidewinder.

Another bait Satan uses to get us away from the Lord is to work to get us to desire the things in this world. It is an old trick. He tried it on Jesus after the Lord's forty days of fasting. Mathew tells us the story this way (4:8, 9): "Again, the devil taketh him up into an exceeding high mountain, and *sheweth him all the kingdoms of the world,* and the glory of them; And saith unto him, 'All these things will I give thee if thou wilt fall down and worship me.'"

If Jesus rejected *all* the kingdoms of the world, then certainly we should reject what little parcel of that same world the Devil offers us. We have seen the sad tale of a beautiful young lady who begins singing in church. Her voice is beautiful and she is a blessing to those worshipping the Lord. Then she begins to yearn for what the world offers a talent like hers. Soon she is entrenched in all that the Devil offers and the admiration of the world is heaped upon her for a short period of time. God is all but forgotten, and the humbleness of spirit is exchanged for the pride of life. All too often, a life like that ends in total ruin. She did not heed the warning: "The highway of the upright is to depart from evil: he that keepeth his way preserveth his soul" (Proverbs 16:17). How many times must this picture of a life be replayed? Pride gets the better of a person in this situation, and it destroys his or her life. The words of the Bible continue to hold true. Proverbs 16:18, 19: "Pride goeth before destruction, and an haughty spirit before a fall. Better it is to be of an humble spirit with the lowly, than to divide the spoil with the proud." How often would a little humility, in the fear of the Lord, have served to protect from such a tragedy.

The fear of the Lord leads to a satisfying life and spares one from much evil. (Proverbs 19:23: "The fear of the Lord tendeth to life: and he that hath it shall abide satisfied; he shall not be visited with evil.") The fear of the Lord is the way to riches and honor and life. (Proverbs 22:4: "By humility and the fear of the Lord are riches, and honour, and life.") Our desire should always be the approval of God and not the honor and praise of people.

We should never stoop to the level of the world. The morals of this present age are at an all-time low. The repetition of violence continually reported across our network news, the illicit sex that is championed in every aspect of our entertainment industries, the dishonesty and corruption evident in our government—all of these bear this truth out. Millions have relaxed their moral standards so far as to have drifted from any semblance of decency.

The apostasy even lives in the churches today. Christians have begun to abandon their once-held beliefs. To many, Jesus is no longer the Son of God, born of a virgin, sinless, crucified, dead and buried, and resurrected. A waywardness is setting in, and casual Christianity is becoming the norm. Many have fallen away and become missing in action. Others have sold out and changed sides altogether. But none of this has caught God off guard.

> *But there were false prophets also among the people,*
> *even as there shall be false teachers among you,*
> *who privily shall bring in damnable heresies, **even***
> ***denying the Lord that bought them**, and bring*
> *upon themselves swift destruction (2 Peter 2:1).*

Many of you may be asking, "Are you talking about lost people or saved people?" Therein lies the problem. It is getting too hard to tell the difference. In way too many instances, Christians are letting themselves fall into sin. Let us remind ourselves of some truths. Romans 12:21: "Be not overcome of evil but overcome evil with good." If we have fallen, we need to recover ourselves quickly. 2 Timothy 2:26: "And that they may *recover themselves* out of the snare of the devil, who are taken captive by him at his will." The word *recover* finds its modern-day use in phrases like "he is a recovering alcoholic." If we have been caught in one of Satan's snares, we need to get back to the old path that the Lord wants us on. It is called the *straight and narrow way.*

It is not good enough to just start well in our Christian walk. We are saved to make it to the end. Matthew 10:22: "And ye shall be hated of all men for my name's sake: but *he that endureth to the end shall be saved.*" Please notice those words. If we are doing an excellent job for the Lord, then the admiration of the world will not be part of our resume. As much as it depends on us, we are to be at peace with all men, but not all men will be at peace with us.

Satan has the scheme to get us off track. First he tries to distract us. Second, he seeks to attract us. Third, he attacks us. There are no problems that are too difficult. There are no trials that are too severe. There are no burdens too heavy. God's grace is sufficient. The Lord lives in us, and greater is He that is in us than he that is in the world. 1 John 4:4: "Ye are of God, little children, and have overcome them: *because greater is he that is in you than he that is in the world.*"

God and Satan are not of equal strength. This is not a fight to the finish. It was finished more than two thousand years ago on a cross on Calvary's hill.

God is far superior to Satan. God made Satan. Jesus (the God Man) conquered death, hell, and the grave, and he defeated Satan. Here is some more great news. The victory that Jesus wrought has been passed on to us!

> *Nay, in all these things **we are more than conquerors** through him that loved us. For I am persuaded, that neither death, nor life, nor angels, nor principalities, nor powers, nor things present, nor things to come, Nor height, nor depth, nor any other creature, shall be able to separate us from the love of God, which is in Christ Jesus our Lord (Romans 8:37-39).*

We must avoid the sinful pleasures of life. That takes discipline. Set boundaries for yourself. Use restraint in all your choices. Stay on the narrow path. Stay in the *middle* of the narrow path. Don't even walk on the edge of the narrow path. Don't be looking at what the world has to offer. Do as the psalmist did! Psalms 101:3: "I will set no wicked thing before mine eyes: I hate the work of them that turn aside; it shall not cleave to me." *Stay away from Satan's territory.*

Chapter Four
HELL

Hell and destruction are before the Lord:
how much more then the hearts of the chil-
dren of men? (Proverbs 15:11)

Hell is a real place. It is not a state of being. It is the eternal prison of torment for all those who choose not to believe Jesus Christ. It is clear that all unbelievers will stand in judgment before the Son of God. Jesus is the One who suffered. Jesus is the One who died. Jesus is the One who forgives if we believe and repent, and Jesus is the One who will judge if we do not believe and repent. God the Father has given that right to Him and Jesus will judge the "dead, great and small" (Revelation 20:12). After He judges, the lost of all time will be tormented there forever.

Eternal punishment did not have to be their end. Had they believed in Him, and on Him, they too could have been saved. That is the sad truth about those who will most certainly spend eternity in hell. Upon reading this book, some will say that there is not enough grace mentioned in these pages. Please, dear reader, understand: hell was not made for man. It was prepared for the angels that followed Satan. Matthew 25:41: "Then shall he also say unto them on the left hand, 'depart from me, ye cursed, into everlasting fire, prepared for the devil and his angels.'" Hell did not have to be any man's destination. God Himself wishes above all that all would be saved. 2 Peter 3:9: "The Lord is not slack concerning his promise, as some men count slackness; but is longsuffering to us-ward, not willing that any should perish, but that all should come to repentance." *There was enough blood to cover the sins of the whole world if the world would have wanted to accept the provision of salvation.*

Those who don't believe in the cross and what it means view the whole story as a bunch of foolishness. 1 Corinthians 1:18: "For the preaching of the cross is to them that perish foolishness; but unto us which are saved it is the power of God." Can you imagine standing before the One who died on that cross for your sins? He looks with eyes of fire at the soul who thought what He did for you was *foolish.* That should make any soul shudder!

To say that hell is not real or is not a real place is to say that the Bible contains errors. But the Bible declares within itself that its very words are from God. 2 Timothy 3:16: "All Scripture is given by *inspiration of God,* and is profitable for doctrine, for reproof, for correction, for instruction in righteousness." God wrote through men to reach mankind.

God cannot lie. Numbers 23:19: "*God is not a man, that he should lie*; neither the son of man, that he should repent: hath he said, and shall he not do it? Or hath he spoken, and shall he not make it good?" Those who are real Christians have unshakable confidence in the Word of God being the Truth. Jesus said (John 17:17): "Sanctify them through thy truth: *thy word is truth.*" God is due all the honor and worship of all His creation, and that includes you and me. The magnitude of His holiness demands it. The depth of the ugliness of our sin demands judgment.

The truth is that hell is the just end for those who will not believe the truth. 2 Thessalonians 2:12: "That they all might be damned *who believed not the truth* but had pleasure in unrighteousness." Another verse filled with immeasurable horror is Revelation 14:10, 11: "The same shall drink of the wine of the wrath of God, which is poured out without mixture into the cup of his indignation; and he shall be tormented with fire and brimstone in the presence of the holy angels, and in the presence of the Lamb; And the smoke of their torment ascendeth up for ever and ever: and they have no rest day nor night . . . "

Hell will be horrible for all who end there. It will not be a gathering place where the "good ol' boys" meet. It is not Satan's domain. He will not be the king in hell. It was prepared *for* him, and he is doing everything he can to stay out. And may I say, dear reader, it should be your goal to avoid it at all cost. Jesus paid the price for you. Believe it!

Some folks think that not everyone who goes to hell belongs there. It comes from the idea that not everybody is all that bad. But, as stated earlier, the unbelievers went to hell because they did not believe the truth.

There are degrees of punishment in hell. Jesus tells us this when He said, in Matthew 11:22: "But I say unto you, It shall be more tolerable for Tyre and Sidon at the day of judgment, than for you." Again, He made the point when He said (Mark 6:11): "And whosoever shall not receive you, nor hear you, when ye depart thence, shake off the dust under your feet for a testimony against them. Verily I say unto you, It shall be more tolerable for Sodom and Gomorrah in the day of judgment, than for that city." It stands to reason that if things can be more tolerable, then they can be less tolerable as well. But who in their right mind could ever be satisfied to be the "best" person in hell? All will be tormented. No one escapes. No one is let out after some length of time. Remember: Revelation 14:11 says, "And the smoke of their torment ascendeth *up for ever and ever*: and they have no rest day nor night." Forever and forever means forever and forever!

THE DREAM

I had a dream of falling into hell. It was the most terrifying dream I ever had. As the dream started, I was falling back and down a well of darkness. I fell faster and faster, and deeper and deeper I went down this well. My fear engulfed me as I expected to hit bottom at any moment. But I simply kept falling. Faster and faster, deeper and deeper, darker and darker. I was petrified. I began to grit my teeth in anticipation of hitting bottom . . . but I just kept falling. My teeth began to break apart in my mouth as I continued to fall. The dream became more hideous. My gums began bleeding as the broken teeth cut into them. And I just kept falling. The sheer horror of this dream intensified until I woke in a sweat—having never hit the bottom. Immediately, I remembered this verse of Scripture, in Matthew 25:30: "And cast ye the unprofitable servant into outer darkness: there shall be weeping and *gnashing of teeth.*"

The world hates the word *repent.* Yet, all must repent. (Luke 13:3:

"I tell you, Nay: but, except ye repent, ye shall all likewise perish.") Jesus taught more on hell than He did on Heaven. After all, it was Jesus who had created it for the angels that rebelled. 2 Peter 2:4: "For if God spared not the angels that sinned, but cast them down to hell, and delivered them into chains of darkness, to be reserved unto judgment . . . "

In Luke 16:19-31, the Lord tells of an eyewitness account of the rich man and Lazarus.

There was a certain rich man, which was clothed in
purple and fine linen, and fared sumptuously every day:

And there was a certain beggar named Lazarus,
which was laid at his gate, full of sores,

And desiring to be fed with the crumbs which fell from the
rich man's table: moreover, the dogs came and licked his sores.

And it came to pass, that the beggar died, and
was carried by the angels into Abraham's bosom:
the rich man also died, and was buried;

And in hell he lift up his eyes, being in torments, and
seeth Abraham afar off, and Lazarus in his bosom.

And he cried and said, "Father Abraham, have mercy on
me, and send Lazarus, that he may dip the tip of his finger in
water, and cool my tongue; for I am tormented in this flame."

But Abraham said, "Son, remember that thou in thy
lifetime receivedst thy good things, and likewise Lazarus evil
things: but now he is comforted, and thou art tormented.

"And beside all this, between us and you there
is a great gulf fixed: so that they which would
pass from hence to you cannot; neither can they
pass to us, that would come from thence."

Then he said, "I pray thee therefore, father, that
thou wouldest send him to my father's house.

For I have five brethren; that he may testify unto them,
lest they also come into this place of torment."

Abraham saith unto him, "They have Moses
and the prophets; let them hear them."

And he said, "Nay, father Abraham: but if one went
unto them from the dead, they will repent."

And he said unto him, "If they hear not Moses
and the prophets, neither will they be persuaded,
though one rose from the dead."

The first thing to notice is that this is not a parable! Jesus calls
Lazarus by name. This is obviously an incident Jesus knew about. The
second thing to notice is that the rich man went to a real place called
hell. Let us take a closer look into the afterlife described here.

1. The rich man was being tormented. He was thirsty. He still
    had desires, but those desires would remain unfulfilled for all
    eternity. Forever and forever the lost of all time will live with
    never being satisfied on any level. The fires of hell will burn
    hot and burn forever.
2. He had his memory. He knew who Lazarus was and he knew
    who Abraham was. All who will be in hell will have memo-
    ries of what could have been.
3. The rich man knew *why* he was in hell. It was because he
    had not repented while on earth. We can see this from his
    conversation with Abraham (16:30). Isn't it interesting that
    the discussion centers on whether they would believe if
    someone rose from the dead?
4. It is of interest that the underworld Jesus describes here
    seems to have different compartments. There is hell, where
    the rich man was being tormented. There was Abraham's
    bosom, where Lazarus was now being consoled. There was
    a vast gulf between these two places that kept both sides
    separated from the other. Even though some would have the
    heart to bring relief to those in hell, that relief would not be
    allowed. Please note, dear reader: no Christian ever wanted
    someone to go to hell no matter the sin. We are the ones
    who understand a little of the *terror of the Lord*. That same
    terror would have been ours to bear had we not trusted and

believed in the Lord at some point in our life. This book is a cry to any who may be lost to believe upon the Lord before it is too late.

When Jesus spoke to the thief on the cross and promised that he would be with Him in paradise that day, the Lord was speaking of the same Abraham's bosom mentioned in His account of the rich man and Lazarus. We know that Jesus did not mean Heaven when He said "paradise" because, after His resurrection, he instructed Mary not to touch Him because He had not yet ascended into Heaven. (John 20:17: "Jesus saith unto her, 'touch me not; for I am not yet ascended to my Father: but go to my brethren, and say unto them, I ascend unto my Father, and your Father; and to my God, and your God.'") This was, of course, three days after He had promised the thief he would be with Him in paradise that very day.

Jesus was the firstfruits of the resurrection. He was to be preeminent in all things. Thus, the Lord was to be the first to go to Heaven in His resurrected body. The Bible says that He led captivity captive. (Psalms 68:18: "Thou hast ascended on high, *thou hast led captivity captive.*") In other words, He brought all those in paradise with Him once He presented Himself to the Father in Heaven.

One final thing to learn from this story is that where we spend eternity depends on the choice to believe or not believe while on this earth. "It is appointed unto man once to die, and then the judgment" (Hebrews 9:27). The proof as to whether we can believe Jesus is wrapped up in His resurrection from the dead.

The world spends so much time and energy trying to figure out the meaning of life. The purpose of life is simple. We are here to meet God before we die. He has made all the arrangements for us. He created us. He died for us to deliver us from the penalty of our sins. He promised we could live with Him forever. He promised that death would not have to be our final lot in life. He proved it by coming out of His grave and promising us that we could have that same life in Him. Once we have discovered that truth for ourselves, we are to spend the rest of our days trying to persuade others of this incredible certainty.

Some feel that simply believing makes it too simple. But that is precisely the plan God has for us. John 3:18: "He that believeth on him is not condemned: but he that believeth not is condemned already *because he hath not believed* in the name of the only begotten Son of God." It is so simple in its essence. But it is a road block to those who want something more intellectual to believe. They want something more religious to do. 1 Corinthians 1:23 says: "But we preach Christ crucified, unto the Jews a stumbling block, and unto the Greeks foolishness."

How sad it is that most find it such a barrier to just believe the simple gospel message of John 3:16: "For God so loved the world, that he gave his only begotten Son, that whosoever believeth in him should not perish, but have everlasting life." The rich man did not believe it. Lazarus did. One is in hell today. The other is in Heaven.

HELL CONTINUES TO GROW

One of the most alarming of Scriptural thoughts is this: hell keeps getting bigger. Isaiah 5:14: "Therefore hell hath enlarged herself and opened her mouth without measure: and their glory, and their multitude, and their pomp, and he that rejoiceth, shall descend into it." Mankind has fought against the idea of dying for six thousand years. Many new sciences are working at a feverish pace to find a way to bring immortality to the human species. We have nanotechnologies, artificial intelligence, biotechnology, genetics, robotics, and synthetic biology, just to mention a few of humanity's attempts to produce longer and longer lifespans. But the efforts remain fruitless in these attempts to lengthen life. The Bible remains true. Psalms 90:10: "The days of our years are threescore years and ten, and if because of strength they are fourscore years yet is their strength labour and sorrow; for it is soon cut off, and we fly away." God said our lifetime would average seventy to eighty years, and that is still where lifespans remain today. There is no averting death, and the power of the grave continues to grow. The scientific advancements that are made to lengthen life are proof of how close the judgment of God has come. The last thing this world needs is sinful man living with still more time to express his depravity.

Most people who die do not die in the Lord. As much as we preachers try to preach those departed souls into Heaven at their funerals, the truth is that most do not know the Lord. And what is worse, He does not know them. Matthew 7:23: "And then will I profess unto them, I never knew you: depart from me, ye that work iniquity." Every time someone dies without the Lord, hell gets bigger. According to the World Health Organization, 56 million people die worldwide in a year. That figures out to about 153,424 people dying every day in this world.

Death levels the playing field. It matters not the amount of glory one may have attained in this life. It does not mean a thing that some may have accumulated some measure of possessions and prestige. It matters not what brilliant displays of splendor may have ordained a life on earth; the power of the grave evens all scores. The cemetery grows, and hell keeps enlarging itself. How foolish to take pride in any advantageous distinctions we may have reaped on this earth. We can take nothing with us. All we truly have when we die is what we did or did not believe about the Lord while here on earth.

How much more important is it that we seek an alliance with that great and good God who has a city waiting for those who believe? It is a city made without hands. It is a place prepared by the Son of God, who will lovingly usher in all who put their trust in Him. In John 14:2, 3, Jesus states it plainly: "In my Father's house are many mansions: if it were not so, I would have told you. I go to prepare a place for you. And if I go and prepare a place for you, I will come again, and receive you unto myself; that where I am, there ye may be also."

The blatant visible expressions of sin in this world break the heart of every Christian who knows better. Adultery is lauded in movies and TV. We have forgotten the horrors of indulging in the sins of adultery and fornication. Living together has become the norm for so many young people today. But the Bible is crystal clear on the subject. Proverbs 5:5: "Her feet go down to death; her steps take hold on hell." Let us remember that hell is never full. Proverbs 27:20: "Hell and destruction are never full; so, the eyes of man are never satisfied."

The pornographers and smut sellers of this world openly brag about their lifestyles. They make their pact with hell in open defiance against the will of God. Those that traffic in these sins are leading many to hell. Proverbs 7:27: "Her house is the way to hell, going down to the chambers of death." Whatever agreement the sinner believes he has with hell will be broken. Isaiah 28:18: "And your covenant with death shall be disannulled, and your agreement with hell shall not stand; when the overflowing scourge shall pass through, then ye shall be trodden down by it."

Porn stars have been legitimized in recent years. They have been held up on prime time TV as the new entrepreneurs of the twenty-first century. There is no shame anymore. Someone well said that the human being is the only animal that blushes and, indeed, is the only one who *needs* to blush. But we do not even blush anymore. Jeremiah 6:15: "Were they ashamed when they had committed abomination? Nay, *they were not at all ashamed, neither could they blush*: therefore, they shall fall among them that fall: at the time that I visit them they shall be cast down, saith the Lord."

Time is running out on sinful man. Judgment is coming. The Lord will return soon. God is patient. God is merciful. God is long-suffering. But God will not be mocked. The Ten Commandments were removed from the schoolroom walls of this country. This was an effort by unregenerate man to forget the things God has said. But hell awaits. Psalms 9:17: *"The wicked shall be turned into hell, and all the nations that forget God."*

Pray Not

What if the Lord were to ask Christians to stop praying for the lost? It is horrifying in its concept. What if God gave the command to stop pleading for the souls of sinners? Jeremiah 7:16: "*Therefore pray not thou for this people*, neither lift up cry nor prayer for them, neither make intercession to me: for I will not hear thee." Have you heard words more frightening than these? As scary as it is to think of openly rebellious people defying God, it becomes all the more terrifying to imagine a time when God might say to the Christians: "Don't intercede anymore for them." When the Lord decides that judgment must come, it will be quick. Psalms 55:15: "Let death seize upon them and let them go down quick into hell: for wickedness is in their dwellings, and among them." Even Jesus ceased praying for the world. John 17:9: "I pray for them: *I pray not for the world*, but for them which thou hast given me; for they are thine." This same Jesus, who had the psalmist pen "let death seize upon them," is the same Jesus who holds the keys to hell. Revelation 1:18: "I am he that liveth, and was dead; and, behold, I am alive for evermore, amen; and have the keys of hell and of death."

Contrary to some opinions, Satan is not the king of hell. He wants absolutely nothing to do with hell. It is a place of torment that was originally created for him and his angels. It is the Devil's ultimate destination, and he is fighting to the death to stay out of it. His time keeps getting shorter; it will soon run out. And the closer he gets to his judgment, the more fiercely he fights. Revelation 12:12: "Therefore rejoice, ye heavens, and ye that dwell in them. Woe to the inhabiters of the earth and of the sea! For the devil is come down unto you, having great wrath, because he knoweth that *he hath but a short time*." However, it is not his wrath that we should fear, but that of the Lamb of God. Matthew 10:28: "And fear not them which kill the body but are not able to kill the soul: but *rather fear him which is able to destroy both soul and body in hell.*" A verse quoted earlier needs repeating. Psalm 2:12: "Kiss the Son, lest he be angry, and ye perish from the way, when his wrath is kindled but a little. Blessed are all they that put their trust in him." (I'll take up this verse in more depth in a later chapter.)

This place called hell is awful. We no longer seem to think so, but that does not change the truth. It burns with fire. Its torments are indescribable. The Bible uses word pictures like "where their worm dies not." Hell is the place where retribution will be carried out for all eternity. It is a place and not just a state of mind. It is a place of unspeakable misery where the fire is never quenched. It will be the just reward for all the reprobate souls who died apart from the Lord through all ages. Each day more die. Each day more slip into this awful storehouse of lost souls.

Our words are a poor attempt to describe that which is beyond description. Jesus warned, in Mark 9:43: "And if thy hand offends thee, cut it off: it is better for thee to enter into life maimed than having two hands to go into hell, into the fire that never shall be quenched." I cannot imagine what it would be like to die in a fire. Remember the people who have been burned at the stake and, just for a moment, dwell upon the horrors of pain they suffered. Now imagine that those fires never cease. The pain never subsides. Forever and forever. That is hell. It is to be avoided at all cost. That is why Jesus died for us. That is His reason for saving us. Blessed be the Name of the Lord!

Chapter Five

— The Anger of the Lord —

*The **fierce anger of the LORD** shall not return, until he have done it, and until he have performed the intents of his heart: in the latter days ye shall consider it (Jeremiah 30:24).*

Thereupon—

There is a certain phrase that is repeated in the Scriptures thirty times: the anger of the Lord. If you include other similar wordings from the Bible such as the anger of my Lord or the fierceness of his anger, the number of occurrences nears a hundred. God's anger is real. Often, His anger is mentioned in conjunction with the word kindled. For instance, in the Psalms: "Kiss the Son, lest he be angry, and ye perish from the way, when his wrath is kindled but a little. Blessed are all they that put their trust in him."

KINDLED

Kindled is a thought-provoking word. The meaning of the word carries the idea of igniting or inflaming. In the case of this verse, the warning is clear. We are not to provoke or arouse the anger and wrath of the Son of God. Boy Scouts are taught to use kindling to start a fire. They are to begin building a fire with dry grass and small sticks so the fire is sure to catch hold and continue to burn. To interpret this verse, then, we are to understand that it is in our best interest to do nothing that might begin to incite the anger of our Lord. We are to be careful that we do nothing that angers Him even a little. Once His anger is kindled, it is going to burn for a while. So what is it that provokes the anger of our Lord?

The first time the phrase "the anger of the Lord" is mentioned in Scripture, it is found in Exodus (4:14): *"And the anger of the Lord was kindled against Moses, and he said, 'Is not Aaron the Levite thy brother? I know that he can speak well. And also, behold, he cometh forth to meet thee: and when he seeth thee, he will be glad in his heart.'"* Moses had been complaining that he could not speak well for the Lord. That made the Lord angry. God is not looking for ability; He is looking for availability. We are in danger of making the Lord angry when we continue to make excuses for why we cannot serve Him. Please don't miss the point that God's anger was kindled toward Moses. In other words, if we are not careful, we are in danger of making our Lord angry. When we disobey Him, we are going to be chastised. Hebrews 12:6: "For whom the Lord loveth he chasteneth, and scourgeth every son whom he receiveth." From this verse, we can see that the Lord loves us but will correct us when we disappoint Him.

There is another story found in the book of Numbers (11:1-6) that helps us understand some of the reasons that He might get angry.

*And when the people complained, it displeased the LORD: and the LORD heard it, and **his anger was kindled**; and the fire of the LORD burnt among them and consumed them that were in the uttermost parts of the camp. And the people cried unto Moses; and when Moses prayed unto the LORD, the fire was quenched. And he called the name of the place Taberah: because the fire of the LORD burnt among them. And the mixed multitude that was among them fell a lusting: and the children of Israel also*

wept again, and said, "Who shall give us flesh to eat? We
remember the fish, which we did eat in Egypt freely; the
cucumbers, and the melons, and the leeks, and the onions,
and the garlick: But now our soul is dried away: there
is nothing at all, beside this manna, before our eyes."

In verse 10 of this passage in Numbers, it tells us that the anger of the Lord was *kindled greatly*. Remember the admonition from Psalm 2: "*Kiss the Son, lest He be angry, and ye perish from the way, when his wrath is kindled but a little.*" If we could perish when He gets a little angry, imagine what is coming when His anger is *kindled greatly*! The Strong's Concordance defines the word angry in this verse as being enraged to the point of breathing hard. That is a mental image we rarely, if ever, have of God today.

Let us make sure there is complete clarity on what is being emphasized in this book. Our Lord is both a God of love and a God of judgment. This book is not an attempt to get its readers to only think of God as angry. That is far from the truth. The observation is that we have *only* thought of God as loving. He is both. We are well served if we remember that truth. Love and justice are equal parts of His righteous character. You cannot have one without the other. We should not preach one without the other. God is all encompassing.

Another point is this: although God may be angry with you, there can still be hope. Salvation is what the Lord wants for all of us. Isaiah 12:1: "I will praise thee: though thou *wast angry* with me, *thine anger is turned away*, and thou comfortest me." This verse leads to the writer extolling his gratitude for being saved. Isaiah 12:2 continues the thought: "Behold, God is my salvation; I will trust, and not be afraid: for the Lord Jehovah is my strength and my song; he also is become my salvation."

Once you have been saved, you will not be afraid. Once saved, however, you begin to really understand the Terror of the Lord. You are saved *to* something and you are saved *from* something. You are saved to live with the Lord forever in Heaven. You are saved from an eternity separated from Him in hell. Once you have been delivered from the penalty and punishment of your sins, you begin to understand how terrifying it would have been to face an angry God.

WHY GOD GETS ANGRY

Let's take a look at a few of the reasons God does get angry. The first way we might stir up His anger is *complaining*. How often do we risk angering our God with our expressions of discontent? We moan and groan and gripe and grumble and, if we are not careful, we develop a real feeling of resentment toward the way we perceive He is dealing with us. This world has its trials, but we are to be of good cheer, for He has overcome the world. John 16:33: "These things I have spoken unto you, that in me ye might have peace. In the world ye shall have tribulation: *but be of good cheer*; I have overcome the world." Complaining majors on the minors and forgets the much more important things in this life. Once we have been forgiven our sins when we believed, the future that is ours in His kingdom will be amazing. That should keep us in good cheer. Matthew 9:2: "And, behold, they brought to him a man sick of the palsy, lying on a bed: and Jesus seeing their faith said unto the sick of the palsy, '*Son, be of good cheer; thy sins be forgiven thee.*'"

Every time we complain, we have forgotten what it really means to have our sins forgiven. We had no right to anything as sinners. God was not obligated to save us. Yet He loved us so much that He would not leave us in our sinful state. We cannot imagine what God has prepared for all of us who love Him. The struggles in this life are temporary, but the blessings of what is to come are eternal. No matter how great an imagination you might have, you cannot possibly conceive what your future holds. Some of the greatest words of the New Testament are found in First Corinthians chapter two, verse nine: "*But as it is written, eye hath not seen, nor ear heard, neither have entered into the heart of man, the things which God hath prepared for them that love him.*" Oh, how incredible our eternity will be! Blessed be the Name of the Lord!

To go a little deeper into this story from Numbers chapter eleven we need to understand what the Bible is describing when it says "the mixed multitude." In some versions, this phrase is translated as "rabble" or "foreigners." In other words, this mixed multitude that got the anger of the Lord stirred up were not Hebrews. These were a group of people who came out of Egypt with Moses and the other Hebrew children. But this mixed multitude did not have a personal attachment to God. And the discontentment of this group rubbed off on the Israelites. The people Moses led allowed their understanding of God to be tainted by people who did not know God at all. Our perception of the Lord should always come from the Bible He gave us. His Word is truth.

Another reason we as Christians can anger the Lord is *allowing ourselves to conform to the world's way of thinking.* All that the mixed multitude wanted to do was to feed their flesh. The Bible is very clear. We are not to spend our lives trying to fulfill the lusts of the flesh. Chasing the things the world chases keeps us from experiencing the wonders of the Spirit of God. Romans 8:5: "They that are after the flesh do mind the things of the flesh, but they that are after the Spirit the things of the Spirit." Worship services throughout our land are dull because the Christians have lived after the flesh all week and then come in to worship the Lord on Sunday. You cannot spend all week in the flesh and expect to touch God's heart in one hour of spiritual activity. The book of Romans goes on to say in 8:8: "So then they that are in the flesh cannot please God." Forgive us, Lord, for the times that we have displeased you by listening to the world.

TAKING GOD SERIOUSLY

It is time that we take seriously His call to separate ourselves from the evils of this present day. *2 Corinthians 6:17:* "Wherefore *come out from among them, and be ye separate,* saith the Lord, and touch not the unclean thing; and I will receive you." What does God mean by the unclean thing? It is a list that certainly includes the TV shows that glorify adultery and fornication and homosexuality and idolatry. It is the movies that use the Lord's name in vain hundreds and hundreds of times. We watch unclean actors using unclean language while we watch filthy images of immorality. We listen to musicians who live immoral lives while singing impure lyrics in degrading songs. The world does not just condone these practices, it promotes all levels of debauchery. These entertainers are people we would never invite into our homes, but we listen to them and watch them pollute our living rooms day and night.

We wonder why we don't have the blessing of God in our families anymore. We wonder why we don't have the same safe country we once enjoyed. It is because we will not separate ourselves from the filth. He said that if we would come out from among them, He would receive us. But if we continue to disobey this command, He will not be with us. Numbers 12:9: "And the *anger of the Lord* was kindled against them; *and he departed.*" How can we continue to make gods out of sports heroes, movie actors, and porn stars and still believe that the true God will not get angry? Deuteronomy 6:14, 15: "Ye shall not go after other gods, of the gods of the people which are round about you; For the Lord thy God is a jealous God among you lest *the anger of the Lord* thy God be *kindled* against thee and destroy thee from off the face of the earth."

ANGER AT THE LAND

In studying the Scriptures on the anger of the Lord, there is another extremely interesting passage that shows God can get angry at the land. Deuteronomy 29:27: "And the anger of the Lord was kindled *against this land,* to bring upon it all the curses that are written in this book." You may be wondering why God would get angry at the land. There are some good reasons. One of those has to do with His mercy. That's right, *his mercy.* When floods or fires or plagues or storms are used by Him, He is giving man a chance to repent. It is His way of letting us know that He is not pleased without bringing the ultimate consequence of His anger, which is death. His curses on the land cause us many hardships, such as loss of homes, loss of money, or loss of worldly treasures. These calamities are allowed by God to get us to examine the wickedness of our ways. We should be allowing God to search our hearts. Psalm 139:23: "Search me, O God, and know my heart: try me, and know my thoughts: And see if there be any wicked way in me."

We have seen this exhibited in recent years in America. You may say, "We have always had disasters." That is true, but now we often seem to have catastrophes that rank in the category of the "worst ever." We all remember hurricanes Katrina and Harvey of recent years. Katrina (2005) was one of the most devastating hurricanes in the history of the United States. It was, at its time, the deadliest hurricane to strike the U.S. in more than seventy-five years. It produced catastrophic damage, estimated at $75 billion in the New Orleans area and along the Mississippi coast—and is still the costliest U.S. hurricane on record. We can still remember the images broadcast each night on the news.

Hurricane Harvey started intensifying to a Category 4 hurricane before making landfall along the Texas coastline. The storm then stalled, its center over the Texas coast for four days, dropping historical amounts of rainfall, more than 60 inches over southeastern Texas. During the reporting of the unusual way that the hurricane just came to a standstill, one nightly commentator observed that "only God could stop a hurricane." The rains caused terrible flooding, and Harvey is the second-most costly hurricane in U.S. history behind Katrina. At least sixty-eight people died from the direct effects of the storm in Texas, *the largest number of direct deaths from a tropical cyclone in that state since 1919.*

America has experienced floods in cities like Nashville, New Orleans, and Houston. In fact, there have been more than twenty floods in the United States since 2001 that have brought significant damage. Add to those disasters the terrible wildfires in our western states, and one must wonder if God is truly angry at the land to get our attention. Attention to what? Our sinful condition and our unwillingness to repent. This does not imply that God was angry with only those particular cities. The judgment is on America, and these calamities affected all of our country.

As if these disasters are not enough, the scientific prognosticators keep warning us of "the big one" to come in reference to earthquakes in California. Also, reports from Yellowstone National Park of wild animals leaving in droves and hundreds of small tremors concentrated over short periods of time seem to foreshadow a disaster that reportedly could destroy America altogether.

We should be looking to the Bible for understanding the things that are happening and the things to come. It seems the "Old Book" is heating up. There is plenty of fire left in its pages. Joshua 23:16: "When ye have transgressed the covenant of the Lord your God, which he commanded you, and have gone and served other gods, and bowed yourselves to them; then shall the anger of the Lord be *kindled* against you, and ye shall perish quickly from off the good land which he hath given unto you."

Where are the pulpits in America crying, "Repent, for the kingdom of God is at hand"? Instead, we have so-called preachers preaching in big churches telling their congregations that God is at peace with them. Jeremiah 6:14 says, "Saying peace, peace when there is no peace." These pulpiteers never confront sin. They don't identify sin. They rarely mention sin. There can be no peace with God when sin stands in the way. To tell anyone that the God of peace is smiling down on them when there is no repentance is an out-and-out lie. Jesus died to make peace between God and man. On the cross, He was made sin. 2 Corinthians 5:21: "For he hath *made him to be sin* for us, who knew no sin; that we might be made the righteousness of God in him." To state it another way, to make a way for us to be at peace with God, the Prince of Peace had to take the wrath of God upon Himself that we could then, and only then, truly be at peace with God.

When the word of God is preached correctly, then sin is declared clearly, and a call to repentance is given in the hope that remorse has been genuinely felt by the sinner. Unfortunately, however, the hearers hear the words, but they sometimes choose to follow their heart instead of the truth. Deuteronomy 29:19, 20: "And it come to pass, when he heareth the words of this curse, that he bless himself in his heart, saying, *I shall have peace, though I walk in the imagination of mine heart,* to add drunkenness to thirst. The Lord will not spare him, but then *the anger of the Lord* and his jealousy shall smoke against that man, and all the curses that are written in this book shall lie upon him, and the LORD shall blot out his name from under heaven."

Our hearts are evil. To follow one's heart is to put that person's eternity at grave risk. Jeremiah 17:9: "The heart is deceitful above all things, and desperately wicked: who can know it?" It is apparent that God is saying we can't imagine the depths to which our heart's wickedness can go. We hear of sheer evil like human trafficking, and we wonder how these things can be. The answer is a desperately wicked heart. We wonder how a person can do some of the things that some people do, and again the answer is: *a heart that is deceitful above all things.*

WHAT GOD HATES

It may still be hard for you to believe that God can get angry, but there is no denying it. There are things He hates. Proverbs 6:16-19: "These six things doth the Lord hate: yea, seven are an abomination unto him; A proud look, a lying tongue, and hands that shed innocent blood, An heart that deviseth wicked imaginations, feet that be swift in running to mischief, A false witness that speaketh lies, and he that soweth discord among brethren." In this one passage of Scripture, the Lord gives us seven things He hates.

1. **A proud look**: There are too many examples of the kind of pride God hates. In keeping with our topic, let this be said: anyone who exalts their opinion above the Word of God makes God a liar and, by default, is making himself or herself a god. There is no greater pride than this. Psalms 145:8: "The Lord is gracious and full of compassion; slow to anger, and of great mercy." Thank God for this verse. It takes a while for the Lord to get angry. But, He will get angry! He hates the proud look!

2. **A lying tongue**: Satan is God's enemy, and Satan is the father of lies. John 8:44: "Ye are of your father the devil, and the lusts of your father ye will do. He was a murderer from the beginning, and abode not in the truth, because there is no truth in him. When he speaketh a lie, he speaketh of his own: for *he is a liar, and the father of it.*" A lie can be terribly destructive. When we lie, we are instantaneously aligning ourselves with the archenemy of God. God hates a lying tongue!

3. **Hands that shed innocent blood**: We have heard the numbers of yearly abortions until we have become desensitized to their horrific meaning. Seventy million babies have been killed in America since Roe v. Wade. Worldwide, there have been many more. We are living in the last days, and these are perilous times. There is a long list of things that will bring the judgment of God. The one to focus on here is that people will be without *natural affection*. You would think that a mother's love for her baby would be at the top of the "natural love" file. But it is not so. Romans 1:31, 32: " . . . without understanding, covenant breakers, *without natural affection*, implacable, unmerciful: *Who knowing the judgment of God*, that they which commit such things are worthy of death, not only do the same, but have pleasure in them that do them." There it is again. Did you see it, dear reader? *The*

judgment of God! They know about it but ignore it! Mothers love themselves more than they love their own babies. *Please see 2 Timothy 3:2-5:*

> *"For men shall be lovers of their own selves, covetous,*
> *boasters, proud, blasphemers, disobedient to parents,*
> *unthankful, unholy, Without natural affection, trucebreakers,*
> *false accusers, incontinent, fierce, despisers of those that*
> *are good, Traitors, heady, high-minded, lovers of pleasures*
> *more than lovers of God; Having a form of godliness,*
> *but denying the power thereof: from such turn away."*

Judgment is coming. 2 Timothy 3:1: "This know also, that in the last days perilous times shall come." They are worthy of death and death is coming. It rides a pale horse and it will scoop up those who are still rebellious and cast them into hell. Revelation 6:8: "And I looked and behold a *pale horse*: and his name that sat on him was *Death, and Hell* followed with him." God hates the shedding of innocent blood. That means that everyone who dies in this judgment is taken straight into hell. Hell follows death in this judgment. The world says there is no hell, but the Bible says there is. Who are you going to believe?

4. **A heart that deviseth wicked imaginations:** In the last twenty years, technology has brought us amazing opportunities for good. But those with wicked imaginations have usurped the good to pollute the world with evil. We have cyberspace called the "dark web," where all manner of evils transpires. With a push of a button, pornography has been made accessible to the world. Human trafficking has been given an advertising platform. Movies can tell great stories, but they also bring us tons of filth. Horrible images are created from the dark hearts and minds of men. We are supposed to control our imaginations. If we find anything that

we may dwell on that is an offense to Almighty God, it is our responsibility to cast down the thoughts. 2 Corinthians 10:5: "Casting down imaginations, and every high thing that exalteth itself against the knowledge of God, and bringing into captivity every thought to the obedience of Christ." We insult Him with our inventions. Jeremiah 8:19: "Why have they provoked me to anger with their graven images, and with strange vanities?" God destroyed the earth once in the days of Noah because of the wicked imaginations of mankind. Genesis 6:5: "And God saw that the *wickedness of man* was great in the earth, and that *every imagination of the thoughts of his heart* was only evil continually." He will come to destroy the earth again.

Knowing, therefore, the *terror of the Lord*, we continue to try to persuade men that they might turn from their wicked ways. If we, as Christians, are going to get the world to listen to us, then our walk with the Lord needs to be impeccable. That will take a real commitment on our part. We should witness to the world and pray for the world, but we are never to partake of the sins of the world. Those in the world are the first to recognize a hypocrite. 2 Corinthians 6:17: "Wherefore come out from among them, and be ye separate, saith the Lord, and touch not the unclean thing; and I will receive you." Either we will separate from the world and draw close to God, or we will separate from God and draw closer to the world. The battle begins in the mind. He hates the heart that devises wicked imaginations!

5. **Feet that be swift in running to mischief:** How many times have we seen this scenario played out in recent years? A policeman shoots someone in the line of duty, and the next thing you know, busloads of people ride to the town from other states to loot and rampage and take advantage of the situation. It always seems that the worst of the mischief is

done through the night. It is as if the perpetrators just can't get enough. The Bible has much to say about this. Proverbs 4:16: "For they sleep not, except they have done mischief; and their sleep is taken away, unless they cause some to fall." Picture this scene. The home team wins the championship game, and the next thing you know crowds are setting fires throughout the town and overturning cars. *Feet that are swift in running to mischief.* There are people who lie awake at night trying to figure a way into more trouble! They have no qualms about carrying out their evil plans. Psalms 36:4: "He deviseth mischief upon his bed; he setteth himself in a way that is not good; he abhorreth not evil." Those who run to mischief pull others into their evil ways. They feel safety and power in numbers, which only promotes worse sins. God hates the feet that are swift to run to mischief.

6. **A false witness that speaketh lies:** There was a time when no one questioned the idea of swearing an oath of truth in a court of law while placing their hand on a Bible. But in these last days, even this act of solemnity has come under attack. The result has been the lack of truth in testimonies. Presidents lie. Congressmen lie. Senators lie. News anchors lie. The truth is harder and harder to discern because so many speak lies. What makes this one different from "a lying tongue" is that the one lying is claiming to be witness to what they are relaying. That gives them more validity—and the evil of their tongue destroys more deeply. When Jesus was on trial, the crowd told lies about Him. The psalmist prophesied the thoughts of Jesus on that day. Psalms 35:11: "False witnesses did rise up; they laid to my charge things that I knew not." It is no wonder that the ninth commandment is to not bear false witness. (Exodus 20:16: "Thou shalt not bear false witness against thy neighbour.") We should have no problem with swearing to tell the truth while our

hand is on the Bible, for it is the book of truth. We should be glad to tell the whole truth with our hand on the book that speaks of Jesus, who *is* the truth. We should be careful to tell nothing but the truth while touching the Scriptures that declare boldly to all: *the truth shall set you free!* God hates a false witness that speaks lies.

7. **He that soweth discord among the brethren:** How many times have we heard the story of a church that splits because two factions within its walls cannot agree? Satan is the master at sowing discord. It started in the garden of Eden. With his slippery forked tongue, he was able to put Adam and Eve at odds with their Creator. He managed to get Cain to kill Abel. He is *still* advancing the hatred that developed between Isaac and Ishmael. He slithered his way into Jacob's family and got Joseph's brothers to sell him into slavery. Satan tries to use those same old tricks in today's churches. The church busybodies begin to stick their noses where they do not belong. They pry and snoop and butt in, chime in, push in, and try to put their two cents in everywhere. Their intrusion is usually sown with words that are less than gracious. The Bible speaks to this: Ephesians 4:29: "Let no corrupt communication proceed out of your mouth, but that which is good to the use of edifying, that it may minister grace unto the hearers." God can't stand the actions of church members who create dissention in the church. He is incredibly displeased when someone breaks up the harmony of a loving body of believers. There is plenty of strife and division in the world. We should put a guard on our tongues. James 1:26: "If any man among you seem to be religious, and bridleth not his tongue, but deceiveth his own heart, this man's religion is vain." We all must learn to control our tongue. It would be good to ask ourselves before we speak: does it even need

to be said? 1 Peter 3:10: "For he that will love life, and see good days, let him refrain his tongue from evil, and his lips that they speak no guile." Jesus said that He spoke nothing of Himself, but only what the Father in Heaven gave Him to say. John 8:28: "Then said Jesus unto them, when ye have lifted up the Son of man, then shall ye know that I am he, and that *I do nothing of myself; but as my Father hath taught me, I speak these things.*"

Maybe we should ask ourselves before we speak: does God want me to say this? If so, does He want me to say it in this way? Remember, He hates the one who sows discord among the brethren!

Hate is a strong word. The Bible says that Cain hated Abel—and look what happened. God does not just dislike these seven things. Although He disapproves of them, it goes deeper than that. The Lord has an open hostility against those who fall guilty to His list. He detests the wicked who take part in the things He hates. He is at extreme enmity with them. Yes, God loves this world. Yes, He sent His Son to this world. But make no mistake. The things He hates, He hates with a passion.

How long will it take for the world to hear? What more must happen to get the attention of a lost and dying generation? This is a stern warning to say we must be listening to God. He will not be ignored forever. He will be heard. If His offer of grace is neglected, He will be heard through His anger in judgment. Isaiah 30:30: "And *the Lord shall cause his glorious voice to be heard*, and shall shew the lighting down of his arm, *with the indignation of his anger*, and with the flame of a devouring fire, with scattering, and tempest, and hailstones."

I believe we are living on borrowed time. The Lord knows perfectly well when He is going to pour out His wrath without measure. His anger will not be on full display yet. He has purposed in His heart to make sure we have a chance to consider what is coming. The prophet Jeremiah put it this way, in Jeremiah 23:20: "The anger of the Lord shall not return, until he has executed, and till he have performed the thoughts of his heart: in the latter days ye shall consider it perfectly." This book is one of many calls to consider the warning completely. Give heed to it. Don't avoid its declarations of approaching danger. Mark it down. Disobedience will lead to punishment.

You are responsible for your soul. This message must be dealt with. What in this world is more important than your soul? Mark 8:36: "For what shall it profit a man, if he shall gain the whole world, and lose his own soul?" Without the marvelous provision of salvation through Jesus Christ, we live life suspended before the anger of the Lord. Jeremiah 51:45: "My people, go ye out of the midst of her, and *deliver ye every man his soul from the fierce anger of the Lord.*" There is no lack of power in our Lord to throw wicked men into hell at any moment. The Lord's eyes are holy eyes filled with fire.

PREACHERS

There has been a disturbing turn of events in the last couple of decades. There was a time when a pastor or minister or priest was given a nod of respect even from the unchurched world. This has changed. That esteem is lacking in today's world. It is true that some of the fault lies with the publicly fallen preachers in the last couple of decades. God has chosen to use sinners to preach to sinners. In other words, He uses men who have been saved by the grace of God to tell others of that same incredible grace. Preachers, like all true Christians, are a new creation in Christ Jesus. (2 Corinthians 5:17: "Therefore if any man be in Christ, he is a new creature: old things are passed away; behold, all things are become new.") At the point of salvation, God sees us as a new creation. We have been *born again.*

The bad news is that we still live in these old sinful bodies. It is true that some have fallen back into some old ways and thereby have ruined their testimony and have dramatically set at nought their power to convince others of the truth that they preach. Oh, what an awful price to pay. Those who have been called to the preaching of the gospel of Jesus Christ have a grave responsibility. Good preachers know the truth. It is their responsibility to declare the truth. But when the time comes—and it seems to be here—when the world no longer respects those who God has called to spread that truth, it puts us on the verge of running directly into the *anger of the lord*. Lamentations 4:16: "The anger of the Lord hath divided them; he will no more regard them: they respected not the persons of the priests, they favoured not the elders."

It is truly regretable that so many preachers and pastors have fallen to various lusts of the flesh. Satan has made sure that this has been observed by the lost world. But preaching is still God's chosen method for spreading the gospel. And preachers are His preferred mouthpiece that some might be saved. How can anyone be saved who has not heard the plan of salvation? How can that be done without a preacher? Romans 10:14: "How then shall they call on him in whom they have not believed? and how shall they believe in him of whom they have not heard? and how shall they hear without a preacher?"

Preachers are not perfect. But this world owes a debt of gratitude to those who fight the good fight to bring this incredible message of hope to anyone who will believe. Thank God that He is slow to anger. But that does not mean He will let the guilty go unpunished. Nahum 1:3: "The Lord is slow to anger, and great in power, and *will not at all acquit the wicked*." Matthew 6:33 says that we are to "seek first the kingdom of God."

Jesus said that "the meek will inherit the earth." If we take both of these verses to heart, we can avoid the anger of the Lord. Zephaniah 2:3: "Seek ye the Lord, all ye meek of the earth, which have wrought his judgment; seek righteousness, seek meekness: it may be ye shall be hid in the day of the Lord's anger."

Isn't it a precious thought that God prefers to hide us with Him while He pours out His indignation upon the nations? It is the preaching of the gospel that stands in the gap between a world that should be punished and a God who would prefer that all be saved. 1 Timothy 2:4: "Who will have all men to be saved, and to come unto the knowledge of the truth."

Chapter Six

His Fury

Behold, a whirlwind of the Lord is gone forth in fury,
even a grievous whirlwind: it shall fall grievously
upon the head of the wicked (Jeremiah 23:9).

T he word fury is used seventy times in sixty-six verses of the Bible. Fifty-seven of the sixty-six verses use the word in direct relation to God's fury. In the Hebrew language, the word is chema. The definition is: heat; fever pitch; bottles; hot displeasure; rage; furious and wrathful. To put this into a simple sentence: God's fury is bottled up in rage, brought to a fever pitch of His hot displeasure that is readied to be dispensed furiously upon the objects of His wrath. Twice in Scripture Jesus asked this question: "Who hath warned you to flee from the wrath to come?" (Matthew 3:7 and Luke 3:7) The preachers of the world need to be warning all who can hear. And those who have ears to hear, let them hear.

Christians know all too well their awful state of rebellion against God before they were saved. They hate that anyone should be condemned. But they also know that without repentance there is no hope for salvation. There has to be a turning away from the sins of our old nature and a heart-changing belief that the blood that Jesus shed on the cross was for us. Hebrews 9:22: "And almost all things are by the law purged with blood, and without shedding of blood is no remission." We must be saved to avoid His fury. The Bible says that we must be born again. We must turn from our wicked ways. This does not mean "turning over a new leaf." It is both a turning away *from* the old sinful ways and turning *to* God through His Son Jesus Christ. 1 Thessalonians 1:9, 10: "For they themselves shew of us what manner of entering in we had unto you, and how ye turned to God from idols to serve the living and true God; And to wait for his Son from heaven, whom he raised from the dead, even Jesus, which delivered us from the *wrath to come*."

REPENTANCE REQUIRED

Many do not want to hear that they must repent. There needs to be a time, however, when the sinner is truly sorry for his sin. Not merely apologetic for what has happened because of his sin but remorseful that his sin was a slap in God's face. No wonder the Lord says this of His fury, in Ezekiel 38:18: " . . . saith the Lord God, that *my fury shall come up in my face*." We need to have the heart of the psalmist when he wrote, in Psalms 38:17, 18: "For I am ready to halt, and my sorrow is continually before me. For I will declare mine iniquity; *I will be sorry for my sin*." There was a time people were sorry for their sin, but we now live in a generation that will not identify any action as sin.

Sinners are their own final authority. They have become their own gods. The Bible should be the final authority. God wrote it. What it says should be the measuring stick for what is sin and what is not.

We have said earlier that our hearts are desperately wicked. We have hard hearts. They are not naturally open to the love of God. The heart is where we make our more profound emotional decisions. It is our heart that we must let God control. When it comes to our responding to the Lord, it is rarely love at first sight. He calls to us to deal with our heart condition. The prophet Jeremiah wrote: "Circumcise yourselves to the Lord, and take away the foreskins of *your heart,* ye men of Judah and inhabitants of Jerusalem: lest *my fury* come forth like fire, and burn that none can quench it, because of the evil of your doings."

CIRCUMCISION

God instituted circumcision in the seventeenth chapter of Genesis. Abraham was to follow the command to circumcise every male child at eight days old. Circumcision was never a guarantee of salvation. It was only to be a sign. Circumcision was the physical evidence that the Hebrews were followers of the true God. The Lord wants our *hearts* to be circumcised. We are to cut away the hardness that prevents us from listening to God and believing in Him. If we are willing to do that, then and only then shall we be saved. However, to not deal with the stiffness in our rebellious attitude toward the Lord is to put ourselves in the direct path of *his fury*. Believing God and loving men is the outward evidence of a heart that is circumcised. God has done away with fleshly circumcision as a sign of righteousness since Jesus has come. Salvation is a matter of the heart that fully trusts in the Lord and does not merely follow rules and regulations. (Acts 4:12: "Neither is there salvation in any other: for there is none other name under Heaven given among men, whereby we must be saved.") It is the Bible. It is the truth.

OPPOSITION TO GOD

Sinners live lives opposed to God. They are inconsistent if not down-right hostile to His ways. Any choice to be contrary to the Lord puts one in dreadful danger of His fury. Leviticus 26:27, 28: "And if ye will not for all this hearken unto me but walk contrary unto me; then I will walk contrary unto you also *in fury*; and I, even I, will chastise you seven times for your sins." God is saying that if you are opposed to Him, then He will be opposed to you. If you are hostile toward Him, He will be hostile toward you. Why would anyone ever want to be in that position? Is your sin really worth that?

Sinners feed their flesh the delicacies of the world. They consume all they can from Satan's buffet table of pride and power and possessions and perversions, never considering the fury of God's wrath. Please, dear reader, listen to the warning. Job 20:23: "When he is about to fill his belly, God shall cast the *fury of his wrath* upon him and shall rain it upon him while he is eating."

You may find this truth about the fury of God hard to comprehend. Remember, though, how long the Lord has held back. He is longsuffering. He has been longsuffering. But His fury has been bottled up a long time. He has been holding back a long time. And when He pours it out, He will pour it all out. And then he will scrape whatever is left in the bottom of His cup of wrath and He will wring out that anger also. Hear the words of the Lord! Isaiah 51:17: "Awake, awake, stand up, O Jerusalem, which hast drunk at the hand of the Lord the *cup of his fury; thou hast drunken the dregs of the cup of trembling, and wrung them out.*"

REBELLION

There is a day coming when the Lord will grow tired of man's rebellion. He will have had His patience exhausted. His tolerance for our insubordinations will have been taken to the limit. What will follow will be full-blown fury. Jeremiah 6:11: "Therefore I am *full of the fury* of the Lord; *I am weary with holding in*: I will pour it out upon the children abroad, and upon the assembly of young men together: for even the husband with the wife shall be taken, the aged with him that is full of days."

God is a God of love. He proved that at the cross of Jesus Christ. Our Lord experienced the full wrath of God against sin as He hung there more than two thousand years ago. He did it because He loves us. He did it alone. He took the full brunt of God's hatred and anger against sin. We deserved it. He suffered it. And He did it willingly. He did it for anyone who would believe that His death could be a substitution for their deserved death.

Many have believed in Him and in what He did. Many more have not. (Matthew 7:14: "Because strait is the gate, and narrow is the way, which leadeth unto life, and few there be that find it.") The strait gate is narrow, but it is not hard to find. Jesus is the way. The fact that He went to the cross alone and suffered alone and was punished alone leads to the day that He will pour out the wrath of God alone. Isaiah 63:3: "I have trodden the winepress alone; and of the people *there was none with me*: for I will tread them in mine anger and trample them in my *fury*; and their blood shall be sprinkled upon my garments, and I will stain all my raiment."

You may be saying, "But this is Old Testament!" So, please listen to the New Testament, from Revelation 19:11-17.

> *And I saw heaven opened and behold a white horse; and he that sat upon him was called Faithful and True, and in righteousness he doth judge and make war. His eyes were as a flame of fire, and on his head were many crowns; and he had a name written, that no man knew, but he himself. And he was **clothed with a vesture dipped in blood**: and his name is called The Word of God. And the armies which were in Heaven followed him upon white horses, clothed in fine linen, white and clean. And out of his mouth goeth a sharp sword, that with it he should smite the nations: and he shall rule them with a rod of iron: and **he treadeth the winepress of the fierceness and wrath of Almighty God.** And he hath on his vesture and on his thigh a name written, KING OF KINGS and LORD OF LORDS.*

This is a description of the Second Coming of the Lord Jesus Christ! The armies that follow Him include all the believers down through the ages. Those on earth are in for the shock of their lives. This is why Jude said, in verse 23 of his book: "And *others save with fear*, pulling them out of the fire; hating even the garment spotted by the flesh."

The fury of the Lord is a real thing. It should strike fear in the heart of anyone who has not yet believed. The fear of the Lord is the beginning of wisdom. If it takes fear to get some to hear, then so be it. It would be wonderful if all would respond to a gospel of compassion. That gospel is so much more beautiful to present. But it is obvious, both scripturally and by observation, that not all are listening to the preaching of a God of love. The emphasis from the pulpits of recent years has been decidedly prejudiced to the approach of presenting God as a loving, tender, gentle, merciful Father who loves His children and only wants the best for them. There is nothing wrong with that message as far as it goes, but it needs to be balanced with the truth that judgment will come upon those who do not believe.

God is not everybody's Father. He is everybody's Creator. At the time that we believe in the Lord's work on behalf of our salvation, we are given entrance to the kingdom of God and are added by the Spirit of adoption into the family of God. It is then that He becomes our Father. Romans 8:15: "For ye have not received the spirit of bondage again to fear; but ye have received the Spirit of adoption, whereby we cry, Abba, Father."

We should be presenting God's character in a healthy balance between His love and His anger, His kindness and His fury, His forgiveness and His judgment. We can see by the Romans 8 Scripture that once we are saved, we no longer have the fear that we had before being saved. But we understand the fear. We understand the terror. And with that understanding we should be motivated to persuade others by reminding them of whom they ought to fear. Listen to the words of Jesus on this point, from Matthew 10:28: "And fear not them which kill the body but are not able to kill the soul: but rather fear him which is able to destroy both soul and body in hell." Those are Jesus' words. If He uses words like *kill* and *destroy* and *hell* in relationship to what God will do, shouldn't we also be willing to use those words in sharing the truth about God's character with others?

There are some people who are lost who have an uneasiness about what happens when they die. They have a certain trepidation that at death judgment may follow. If we neglect to preach and teach this part of the gospel that warns of the judgment to come, we are not fulfilling our obligation to be watchmen on the walls. The consequence of this practice is that the world develops a false sense of security. They convince themselves that if there is no judgment, there can be no hell. They rationalize that if there is no final punishment to concern themselves with they are free to do whatever their conscience deems appropriate.

Looking at our society today in comparison to a few decades ago, we can readily see that man's behavior is getting worse. It used to be that the worst thing going on in our schools was gum chewing, running in the halls, and maybe a few pranks that would land a kid in the principal's office. The mass murder of schoolchildren was unheard of until the recent onslaught of terrible events. Public schools have become so unruly that in many instances students are graduating without knowing how to read or write. Often, teachers are relegated to the position of glorified babysitters, and they are simply trying to keep the peace in their classrooms.

SAD STATISTICS

We now have a whole slew of agencies that bring us yearly reviews of the problems plaguing our schools. This annual report produced jointly by the Bureau of Justice Statistics and National Center for Education Statistics presents data on school crime from the perspectives of students, teachers, and principals. In a recent report, it gave twenty-three indicators of school crime and safety, including: violent deaths; nonfatal student and teacher victimization; school environment; fights, weapons, and illegal substances; fear and avoidance; discipline; and security measures. Some of the sources of this information included the National Crime Victimization Survey and its School Crime Supplement report, the Youth Risk Behavior

Surveillance System, the School Survey on Crime and Safety, and the School and Staffing Survey.

In 2016, students ages 12 to 18 experienced 749,400 victimizations (theft and nonfatal violent victimization) at school and 601,300 victimizations away from school. The total victimization rates were 29 victimizations per 1,000 students at school and 24 per 1,000 students away from school. In 2016, the rate of total victimization at school was higher for males (38 of these incidents per 1,000 male students) than for females (20 per 1,000 female students).

During the 2015-2016 school year, the percentage of public schools that reported student bullying occurring at least once a week was higher for middle schools (22 percent) than for high schools (15 percent), combined schools (11 percent), and primary schools (8 percent).

The percentage of public schools that had a plan in place for procedures to be performed in the event of a shooting increased, from 79 percent in 2003-2004 to 92 percent in 2015-2016.

We never used to talk about rampant bullying, and this now includes, of course, the use of the Internet. Today's conversations center on drugs and weapons and shootings. Things have definitely gotten worse rather than better. It is time the preachers get angry and the preaching gets hotter. This is no time to mince words while trying to be politically correct. We took the Ten Commandments (which includes "Thou shalt not kill") off the walls of our schools. It is time to put them back! Let's ask a simple question. What is more dangerous to our schoolchildren? Is it worse to have the Ten Commandments hanging on the walls of our schools or to have murderers running those same halls? When we had the first, we did not have the second.

SORCERIES

Sorceries is a word used in the Bible more often than you might at first think. One example is found in Revelation 9:21: "Neither repented they of their murders, nor of their *sorceries*, nor of their fornication, nor of their thefts." *Strong's Concordance* gives the Greek word for sorceries as *pharmakeia*. It is the word we get *pharmacy* from in English. Its definition includes words like drugged, medication, sorcery, and witchcraft. *Strong's* even mentions "poisoner." The list of names of mood-altering drugs would fill up this page. Heroin is on the increase again, as are cocaine and marijuana.

PRESCRIPTION DRUGS

More people are on prescription drugs than ever before. In fact, there is a nationwide epidemic of drug addiction taking place in America. People are overdosing and dying from prescription narcotics at an alarming rate. Teens are abusing drugs they have stolen from their parents or are getting from their friends on the street. More and more parents and young adults are turning to the streets to buy illegal drugs like heroin because of an initial addiction to medication that they were prescribed legally. Doctors are at a point where they don't want to prescribe certain drugs because of the hassles they must face with the federal Food and Drug Administration. About 115 Americans die each day from opioid overdose, according to the Centers for Disease Control and Prevention. This massive spike in the last few years has prompted nearly thirty states to pass laws governing how long patients can get opioids and/or how strong a daily dose can be. Some require long-term users to submit to pill counts or urine tests that often aren't covered by insurance. In the private sector, liability worries have some pharmacies refusing to stock opioids altogether, while some insurers have said they will limit the doses.

Pharmaceutical companies produce more prescription drugs than our population can consume, and the population consumes a *lot* of these drugs. Prescription drug abuse is on the rise in every area of society. A report from the Maryland Addiction Recovery center lists the top 10 abused prescription drugs:

1. **OxyContin.** OxyContin is a narcotic pain reliever used to treat moderate to severe pain. Pressure from the Federal Drug Administration has resulted in the medical community's resistance to even prescribing this drug. Street values surge higher and become exceedingly profitable as the demand for illegal access increases.

2. **Xanax.** Xanax is a medication used in the treatment of anxiety and panic disorders. Xanax is often abused with alcohol, sometimes causing the user to black out and forget events that took place while they were high on the drug. Detox and withdrawal from Xanax is dangerous and can be fatal if not medically treated.

3. **Vicodin.** Vicodin is a narcotic pain killer prescribed for relief of moderate to moderately severe pain. While often touted as less harmful for abuse than OxyContin or Percocet, there are newer, stronger, potent versions of the drug now hitting the market.

4. **Suboxone.** Suboxone is a prescription drug created as a treatment of opioid dependence and was initially planned as a bridge for a patient with the goal of abstinence from drugs. It is an effective drug used to aid in the detox process for a patient addicted to heroin or other prescription drugs. It is now often sold on the streets and has become the number one illicit drug bought and sold in jails and prisons in the United States. In other words, we have people getting hooked on a drug that was supposed to help them get *off another drug* they were addicted to in the first place.

5. **Adderall.** Adderall is a drug used in the treatment of attention deficit hyperactivity disorder (ADHD) and in the treatment of narcolepsy. Narcolepsy is a long-term neurological disorder that involves a decreased ability to regulate sleep-wake cycles. Adderall is widely known as being abused on

college campuses to aid students in studying and focusing, as well as being abused by those in high-stress jobs. Adderall is often prescribed to adolescents. The plague of addiction is being passed down to our children. (Isaiah 47:9: "But these two things shall come to thee in a moment in one day, *the loss of children*, and widowhood: they shall come upon thee in their perfection *for the multitude of thy sorceries*, and for the great abundance of thine enchantments.")

6. **Valium.** Valium is a prescription medication used to treat anxiety disorders, alcohol withdrawal symptoms, or muscle spasms. It is often overprescribed or incorrectly prescribed for addiction patients. Valium has been found to be abused along with alcohol or other depressants.

7. **Percocet.** Percocet is another type of narcotic painkiller. It is a combination of opioid analgesic and aniline analgesic for relief of moderate to moderately severe pain. It is often crushed into a powder and snorted for a quicker high.

8. **Ambien.** Ambien is a sedative used for the short-term treatment of insomnia. It aids a patient in falling asleep or staying asleep. It is often abused in conjunction with other drugs or to help a person in coming down from a high on drugs such as crack, cocaine, or crystal meth.

9. **Fentanyl.** Fentanyl was created to assist in management of breakthrough pain in adults with cancer who had already routinely taken other opioid medicines on a regular schedule. Often Fentanyl is administered by a patch or lollipop. Most recently, a rash of heroin overdose deaths throughout the country was found to be caused by heroin that was cut with Fentanyl.

10. **Klonopin.** This drug was created for management of seizures in children as well as adults. It is used for the treatment of panic disorder and is often abused in conjunction with Adderall or alcohol.

Most Americans have become quite familiar with the names of some or all of the drugs mentioned above, and more. It we are not using them, we may have, or we know someone close to us who is using one of these prescriptions. The point is this: *they have become increasingly prevalent throughout our culture.* Their mention has become second nature in relevant conversations. We have accepted with ease the use of medications for almost any medical problem.

There is no question that there are good people taking correct doses of prescription drugs for legitimate health reasons. Many of the legitimate patients are struggling to get their prescriptions filled due to the opioid epidemic. This list of drug names is given to show how comfortable we have become with the drugs and medications prevalent in the pharmaceutical community. The problems arise when individuals begin to misuse the prescriptions for their fleshly benefit or they are illegally sold to people who have developed an addiction to one or more of these. Remember, the verse in Revelation 9 said they "did not repent" . . . "of their sorceries." They would not stop. Drug dealers keep dealing and addicts keep using.

As if illegal drugs and misuse of legal drugs is not enough, mankind continues to try and develop stronger synthetic chemicals in its never-ending attempt to find a "better high." One of the newer and more deadly drugs to come along is called Flakka. Flakka is a designer drug that can be snorted, smoked, injected, or swallowed. It may also be combined with other softer drugs such as marijuana. It is often taken with the use of e-cigarettes. The effects of this drug on the user are sometimes diabolical. We have read the news or seen images of maniacal behavior. There have been demonic attempts by some on this drug to attack and try to *eat the flesh* from another human being. If God does not bring His judgment on this world, then this is the behavior that will ever increase in its horrors.

Drug abuse is not just a problem in America, but around the world. It will continue to be a curse until the Lord takes the church away in the rapture and then begins to pour out His wrath. Revelation

18:23: "And the light of a candle shall shine no more at all in thee; and *the voice of the bridegroom and of the bride shall be heard no more at all in thee*: for thy merchants were the great men of the earth; for *by thy sorceries were all nations deceived.*"

The unsaved world does not want the Lord Jesus Christ as its king. The words from two thousand years ago are branded on their hearts. Luke 19:14: "But his citizens hated him, and sent a message after him, saying, we will *not have this man to reign over us.*" But reign He will. Every knee will bow, and every tongue will confess, that Jesus Christ is Lord!

The unsaved world hates to hear those words. They hate the Bible. They hate to be reminded of what it says. They do all they can to discredit the Word of God. According to *USA Today* (April 23, 2018), GQ magazine (a book of "grooming" tips, gadget suggestions, and style advice) has sparked a social media frenzy by calling the Christian Holy Bible "foolish, repetitive, and contradictory" and placing it on a list of "Twenty-One Books You Don't Have to Read. . . . *The Holy Bible* is rated very highly by all the people who supposedly live by it but who have not read it," novelist Jesse Ball wrote in GQ in the spring of 2018. "Those who have read it know there are some good parts, but overall it is certainly not the finest thing that man has ever produced." The article goes on to say that the magazine finds the Bible "repetitive, self-contradictory, sententious (using pompous language), foolish, and even at times ill-intentioned."

The Bible is supernatural in its existence. Man did not write this book. God did. 2 Timothy 3:16: "*All scripture is given by inspiration of God*, and is profitable for doctrine, for reproof, for correction, for instruction in righteousness." God inspired forty different men over 1,600 years to write down His Word. In fact, men are warned in Scripture to not add to or take away any of the words written in the Book. Deuteronomy 4:2: "Ye shall not add unto the word which I command you, neither shall ye diminish ought from it, that ye may keep the commandments of the Lord your God which I command you." This warning to men is so important that it is given again in the New Testament, in Revelation 22:19: "And if any man shall take away from the words of the book of this prophecy, God shall take away his part out of the book of life, and out of the holy city, and from the things which are written in this book." To say there are "some good parts" implies that the other parts need to be changed or done away with altogether.

How sad to think that those who so oppose the Bible will have no part in Heaven. They hated the book of His Word, so God will take away their part in the Book. The Bible was not ill-intentioned. It tells everyone of God's plan to bring us to Heaven. It convicts men and women of their sin that we might repent and ask forgiveness. It conveys the very heart of God toward us in that, while we were still sinners, He had already designed a marvelous plan to take our place for the punishment that had to be administered against sin. The Bible is a great story, cover to cover, about Jesus the very son of God. It is a book that God intends to save us with and to give us all that He has in His kingdom. It describes the plan by which He would bring us back to Himself. The design of His purpose is marvelously woven through the pages of scriptures from Genesis to Revelation. It was His *full intention* to accomplish all of His purpose in the person of Jesus Christ!

Repetitive? You bet! The central message needs to be repeated over and over and over again. Generation after generation has passed down the same story. It should be repeated every Sunday, every day, every hour that some might truly hear and be saved. Revelation 3:6: "He that hath an ear, let him hear what the Spirit saith unto the churches." If they will not hear, the Lord will give them what they deserve based on what they did. Isaiah 59:18: "According to their deeds, accordingly he will repay, fury to his adversaries, recompence to his enemies; to the islands, he will repay recompence."

Take heed, dear reader. If you have not repented and called upon the name of the Lord, then you will be judged for all that you have done. Earlier, it was stated that anyone who rejected God's plan through His Son would be excluded from the book of life. Revelation makes it extremely clear that the sentence will be handed out at the Great White Throne judgment. Revelation 20:12: "And I saw the dead, small and great, stand before God; and the books were opened: and another book was opened, which *is the book of life*: and the dead were judged out of those things which were written in the books, *according to their works*." Add to that, Revelation 20:15: "And whosoever was not found written *in the book of life* was cast into the lake of fire."

Heed the warning before it is too late. Flee from the wrath to come!

CHAPTER SEVEN
'KISS THE SON,
—— LEST HE BE ANGRY' ——

Therefore thus saith the Lord God: I will even rend
*it with a stormy wind in **my fury**; and there shall*
*be an overflowing shower in **mine anger**, and great*
*hailstones in **my fury** to consume it (Ezekiel 13:13).*

We have quoted Psalm 2:12 earlier in this book. Let's revisit this critical verse in depth. The full verse reads:

> *Kiss the Son, lest he be angry, and ye perish from*
> *the way, when his wrath is kindled but a little.*
> *Blessed are all they that put their trust in him.*

It has long been debated which of two ways is the better approach when it comes to trying to win souls. Some preachers have chosen the more threatening path of communicating the gospel while others have preferred the subtle and loving method of sharing the message of Jesus Christ. Quite frankly, both have had a strong scriptural basis to back up their respective ways of reaching sinners with the plan of salvation. Some ministers of the gospel have thundered forth their proclamations using many good Scriptures like the one found in Isaiah 66:15: "For, behold, the Lord will come with fire, and with his chariots like a whirlwind, to render his anger with fury, and his rebuke with flames of fire."

Those who have chosen the gentler appeal also have great Scriptures to choose from, such as Jude 1:21: "Keep yourselves in the love of God, looking for the mercy of our Lord Jesus Christ unto eternal life." It is the contention of this author that both are effective, and both should be used. I am not saying there is too much preaching on the love of God, but I am saying there is not enough preaching on the consequences of sin.

Remember the story of Jacob and Esau? It is a prime example of how a kiss can change hatred into love. You will remember that Jacob had tricked his father, Isaac, into giving to Jacob the blessing that belonged to Esau. That, of course, made Esau extremely angry, to the point that he pledged to kill his brother Jacob. Genesis 27:41: "And Esau hated Jacob because of the blessing wherewith his father blessed him: and Esau said in his heart, 'The days of mourning for my father are at hand; *then will I slay my brother Jacob.*'" Several years passed before the fateful confrontation of the two brothers. As they approached each other, the fear of reprisal and the hatred of betrayal melted with a single kiss. Genesis 33:3, 4: "And he (Jacob) passed over before them, and bowed himself to the ground seven times until he came near to his brother [Esau]. And Esau ran to meet him, and embraced him, and fell on his neck, and *kissed him*: and they wept." At that moment, the two brothers were reconciled to each other.

The kiss of love and acceptance that Esau and Jacob shared is the kiss the psalmist is calling you and me to give to the Son of God. It is a grateful offering of genuine emotion as our fear of the Lord meets His hatred of sin at a place where all is forgiven. Jesus has the right to be angry but offers first His grace and mercy. His grace gives us things we do not deserve. Psalms 78:38: "But he, being full of compassion, forgave their iniquity, and destroyed them not: yea, *many a time turned he his anger away*, and did not stir up all his wrath. The list of blessings is endless. Blessings of Heaven, forgiveness, and life everlasting are ours as gifts from Him. His mercy withholds from us the things we *do* deserve. The penalties for our sins are paid in full by Him. The punishments in an eternal hell are banished from us forever. But for those who refuse to believe in what He did for them, He reserves His wrath. Jeremiah 10:10: "But the LORD is the true God, he is the living God, and an everlasting king: *at his wrath, the earth shall tremble*, and the nations shall not be able to abide his indignation."

Anger and love are both contained in God's character, and they are not incompatible. If God were to say He loves me yet not give or do anything to show that love, I would not believe He loved me. Likewise, if He did not get angry when I disobeyed Him, neither would I believe that He really cares.

The word *kiss* is an expression of love. The command to "kiss the Son" is God expressing to us our duty to show real affection toward Jesus His Son. This deep connection with Him is not possible unless our heart has truly been repentant. Recognizing how distant and separated we were from Him while we were yet sinners helps us draw into a profound connection with Him. We are to express our love and affection to Him lest He be angry and His wrath is kindled but a little. For Jesus to get angry, truly angry, just a little would cause us to perish. In other words, He does not have to get all that violent for us to be completely destroyed. That truth should give us pause to think. And we should think seriously about the ramifications of our actions.

RESTORATION

The kiss is a kiss of restoration. Remember, this kiss can only come after our repentance. It is us telling Him thank you for taking our sins and the penalty of our sins from us. It is an emotional gesture of gratefulness to Him for rectifying a horrible situation. It is not a kiss of appeasement in which we are trying to buy off His wrath. It is not an act of concession on our part to pacify His fury. That would intimate that we might return to our old rebellious ways as soon as He relented. Remember that Judas literally kissed the Son—but his was a kiss of treachery.

This is a kiss to thank Him for reestablishing the relationship between God and us. He was not indebted to us in any way. We were guilty of breaking the bond with our Creator. Before His wrath would come, He offered mercy. This is His love. We approach with thanksgiving to kiss the Son in humble adoration for what He chose to do for us.

Shame on anyone who would snub the opportunity to show this kind of affection toward the Lord. He could have skipped the cross and gone straight to His declaration of Jeremiah 21:5: "And I myself will fight against you with an outstretched hand and with a strong arm, even in *anger*, and in *fury*, and *in great wrath*." This verse gives us more insight into what the Psalmist means when he says, "*His wrath is kindled but a little*."

Praise be to God that this verse, and others, are not meant for Christians. If we are safe in the arms of our Lord, then we are kept from the wrath to come. Romans 8:1: "There is therefore now no condemnation to them which are in Christ Jesus, who walk not after the flesh, but after the Spirit." But those who are not in Christ Jesus and willingly continue to sin have only judgment to look forward to. Hebrew 10:26, 27: "For if we sin willfully after that we have received the knowledge of the truth, there remaineth no more sacrifice for sins, But a *certain fearful looking for of judgment* and fiery indignation, which shall devour the adversaries."

Part of what the Lord restored to us was the removal of the enmity that stood between Him and us. We were separated from Him because of our sin, but He broke down that wall between us. He did that work at the cross, and the benefit of what He did was then transferred to us upon our belief and acceptance of Him. At salvation, we are no longer alienated from Him. The hostility that once existed was wiped away. When two people are enemies, we say that there is "bad blood" between them. To coin the phrase, there was "bad blood" between Jesus and us. He solved that issue by use of His perfect blood. Jesus put it this way (Matthew 26:28): "For this is my blood of the new testament, which is shed for many for the remission of sins." The hymn writer asked and answered the question: "What can wash away my sin? *Nothing but the blood of Jesus!*"

LOYALTY

Christ requires all of us who name His name to yield to His authority. His rules are not just a set of guidelines; they are commandments. When He says we are to love God with all our heart, mind, and soul, He means it. That takes loyalty. The kiss of loyalty expresses our devotion to Him. It is an outward act of an inner sincerity that says to Him, "You can rely on me." Today's brand of Christianity can't get the average Christian to church two Sundays in a row. That does not show much of a bond with our Savior.

It is the hope of this book that there are hearts who want to hear the whole truth. The Lord is searching for souls who are hungering and thirsting after his righteousness. The love of the Lord can motivate our zeal. The Terror of the Lord can also inspire us. Loyalty to Him gives us singleness of mind. Loyalty says that we will honor Him with our whole being. Loyalty says I will restrain myself from evil. Spirit control needs to propel us to self-control. It is most definitely time that we are roused from our slumber. The Lord is coming back soon, and He is bringing His holy angels with Him. Loyalty says that we will not be ashamed of Him. Mark 8:38: "Whosoever, therefore, shall be ashamed of me and of my words in this adulterous and sinful generation; of him also shall the Son of man be ashamed, when he cometh in the glory of his Father with the holy angels."

The call is for us to detach ourselves from this world. We are to disconnect with anything that hinders our obedience to the Lord. 2 Corinthians 6:17: "Wherefore come out from among them, and be ye separate, saith the Lord, and touch not the unclean thing; and I will receive you." Many Christians seemingly do not have the backbone to stand against their own flesh. Statements like "the spirit is willing, but the flesh is weak," are used as an excuse to give in to the sinful nature. Others find it more and more difficult to differentiate between what is sin and what is not. There is a scriptural command that makes this problem easily solved: 1Thessalonians 5:22: "Abstain from all *appearance* of evil." This is easy. If it looks wrong, don't do it. There are a lot of things that the world sees as wrong for Christians. And, in many cases, what they think a Christian should not be doing is not directly prohibited in Scripture. Having an occasional drink is an example. The Bible is clear that we are not to get drunk. A glass of wine with dinner, however, seems to be a different category. Timothy was instructed by Paul to take a little wine for his stomach's sake. (1Timothy 5:23: "Drink no longer water but use a little wine for thy stomach's sake and thine often infirmities." As a Christian, however, if our freedom in the Lord is a stumbling block to another Christian or a lost person, we are instructed to refrain. Abstain means to pass it up. The Lord should be able to trust us. And we should honor that trust. Let us be so diligent concerning our behavior that we do not provide any opportunity for a weaker brother in Christ to fall. And even more, let us not give a lost person the excuse to point fingers and say, "Well, that Christian did it." Romans 14:13: "Let us not therefore judge one another anymore: but judge this rather, that no man put a stumbling block or an occasion to fall in his brother's way."

So here is the question. Are we more loyal to ourselves and our rights or are we more loyal to the Lord Jesus Christ? Have we forgotten how horrible the condition of someone not yet saved really is? Have we forgotten the Terror of the Lord? Where is our allegiance? Christians are guilty of sitting on the fence too often. They are also guilty of sitting on their hands instead of reaching out to the lost. We need the Holy Spirit to help us realign our loyalties. What if the Lord asks us to shun some action or activity in the hope that we would be a better witness? Have we forgotten how incredible it was for us the day we were saved? If we are truly tied to our Savior, then we will have His heart. He wishes above all that men would be saved. What a little thing it is to give up some "right" of ours that one person might come to the knowledge of salvation! The magnitude of the importance in Heaven that someone comes to Christ cannot be overstated. Listen to Jesus' heart, in Luke 15:10; "Likewise, I say unto you, there is joy in the presence of the angels of God over *one sinner* that repenteth." If there is joy in Heaven, there ought to be joy in our hearts.

There is a statement used in Christianity that goes like this: If Jesus is not *Lord of all*, then He is not *Lord at all*. The verse in Psalms chapter two we are reflecting on says we are to kiss *the Son*. He is the Son of God. He is King. He is the judge. He is the savior of our souls and of the world. There truly is no hope outside of Jesus Christ. He knows all things, created all things, owns all things—so why would we not willingly make Him supreme over all things that pertain to our lives? To abstain from all appearance of evil demands that whenever we are faced with a "should we or shouldn't we?" situation, we would be honored to defer to His will and not our will. Obey is not a four-letter word.

There is another quote that we would do well to comply with: *practice what we preach!* We are to follow Him. Matthew 16:24: "Then said Jesus unto his disciples, if any man will come after me, let him deny himself, and take up his cross, and follow me." He is calling us to a deeper attachment to Him than just a casual friendship. He wants us to cleave to Him. Whatever it takes to tear ourselves away from the grip of this world, we are to do. "*Let him deny himself.*" The Lord needs to see by our actions that He may know He can rely on us. This comes when we are consecrated to Him. How many blessings are we missing from our Lord because He cannot yet trust us fully? Our lives should show forth a consistent dedication to His will and His way. When we abide by His word and keep His commandments, we show Him a genuine love and respect. All we who name the name of the Lord want to hear those precious words: "*Well done, thou good and faithful servant: thou hast been faithful over a few things, I will make thee ruler over many things: enter thou into the joy of thy Lord*" (Matthew 25:21). Wouldn't it be nice if, in addition, He were to add, "I was able to depend on you."

TRANSFORMATION

The world needs to see Christians who have cut ties with all the evils that surround us. We who love God need to faithfully follow Him. If our sins are pardoned, they need to be hated. We do not need to live a cut-and-paste Christianity: plugging in a little good here and deleting a little bad there. We need to not conform, but to be transformed. Romans 12:2: "And be not conformed to this world: but be ye transformed by the renewing of your mind, that ye may prove what is that good, and acceptable, and perfect, will of God." We are to be transformed that we might show forth what is the *perfect will of God.* Too many of us are content to live in His permissive will, but all too few are willing to seek to live in His perfect will.

This transformation that the Lord is talking about is a revolutionary process. It is a complete change where "if any man be in Christ, he is a new creature: old things are passed away; behold, all things are become new" (2 Corinthians 5:17). In its essence, it is as radical a change as the Lord's transfiguration. To go from lost to saved, from old to new, from conformed to transformed touches the hem of the miracle transfer when the Son of Man was transfigured into the visible glory of the Son of God. Oh, what a marvelous truth to know that He is in us! Jesus prayed that wonderful prayer, found in John 17:23: "I in them, and thou in me, that they may be made *perfect* in one; and that the world may know that thou hast sent me, and hast loved them, as thou hast loved me." There is that word—perfect— again. It is what He wants for us. It is what He wants in us. It is the perfecting work of the Holy Spirit. He has yanked us from darkness into His marvelous light. Colossians 1:13: "Who hath delivered us from the power of darkness, and hath translated us into the kingdom of his dear Son." Can we do anything less than share this amazing truth with those around us?

Now let us remind ourselves of what is at stake. It is the eternity of lost souls. Who brought you to the Lord? How many people did God use to influence you and be a witness before you? What would have happened to you if they had decided to be less committed to Him? Where would you be today? Where would you be headed? Where would you be spending eternity?

Those around us who have not yet come to the Lord are in desperate trouble. They don't know it. They don't believe it. They may not even care. But we know it and we believe it. And we need to care. We are aware of the Terror of the Lord even though they are not. We should want to live in such a way that we might persuade some.

THE KISS OF ADORATION

Idolatry is the worship of other gods. Even today we seem to continue the practice of kissing the god that we adore. How many times have we witnessed some sports figure, with tears in his eyes, hug and kiss the trophy that has just been won? Whether it is the Stanley Cup or the Masters green jacket or the Super Bowl ring, it is truly sad to watch lost athletes give worship to the only god they know. It is not wrong to compete. It's not wrong to be the best you can be. But the Lord is very clear. *Thou shalt have no other gods before me!* (Exodus 20:3) He goes on to clarify His command. Exodus 20:23: "Ye shall not make with me gods of silver, neither shall ye make unto you gods of gold." In the days of Moses God brought tremendous difficulty to the people who disobeyed His command. Exodus 32:35: "And the Lord *plagued* the people, because they made the calf, which Aaron made." In describing the word "plagued," *Strong's Concordance* uses words like: inflict, hurt, slay, smite down, and put to the worse. God was not just displeased, He took action against the ones He was unhappy with. The Bible says that He (Jesus Christ) "is the same yesterday, and today and forever" (Hebrews 13:8). Malachi 3:6: "For I am the Lord, I change not." Our God is a loving, caring, patient God, but unrepentant sin will not go unpunished.

We should give Him the kiss of adoration. Not a tip of the hat or a nod of the head, but an opening of the heart—this is true worship. How many enter church each Sunday and sing a few songs, sit and listen to the sermon, and then leave, having never come into real worship? How many attend and never sing along and rarely listen to the message? After politely laughing at the obligatory opening humorous story offered by the speaker, the attendees (I hate to call them worshipers) ease back in their pews and drift off into whatever thoughts they would rather embrace.

True worship would begin at the front door of the church. The psalmist said that we should enter His gates with thanksgiving in our hearts, and that we should enter His courts with praise (Psalms 100:3). When we sing we should offer the words of our mouth as prayers to the Almighty. We need to be prepared to allow the Holy Spirit to lift us, convict us if required, and usher us into the presence of our God. We should worship Him in spirit and in truth, and we should be careful not to do anything that might hinder another from that same honor and pleasure.

Many times during a service today, distractions keep those who would worship from being able to do so. Pages are ruffled, children are squirming, others make trips to the bathroom, and often at the most inopportune times. It is a wonder that anyone's heart ever has a chance to be convicted. There are legitimate times when things will happen and need to be addressed during a service. But whatever happened to the *solemn assembly?* Joel 1:14: "Sanctify ye a fast, call a *solemn assembly,* gather the elders and all the inhabitants of the *land into the house of the Lord your God,* and cry unto the Lord."

There are some in this generation of churchgoers who seem to have lost any sincere desire to hear the Word of God. We seem to be in a quandary. Is it because apostasy has entered the hearts of the hearers, or is it because the sermons have lost their zeal? It is perplexing, to say the very least, because the Word of God is as relevant and exciting as it has ever been. It should be as important to us as it was in the days of Ezra and Nehemiah.

Nehemiah was a cupbearer for the Persian king Artaxerxes I when the Medo-Persian empire ruled over God's people. He had a position of great responsibility and was a trusted adviser to the king. He secured the permission of Artaxerxes to rebuild the walls of Jerusalem. While Nehemiah was primarily concerned with the physical restoration of the walls of his nation, Ezra dealt with the spiritual restoration of Judah. The following is from the book of Nehemiah, and it shows how important the Word of God was to God's people at that time. Ezra called together one of the largest church services ever. According to Nehemiah 7:66, there were 42,360 in attendance. The following is a tremendous passage, from Nehemiah 8:1-8. (Each paragraph in the following corresponds to one verse.)

And all the people gathered themselves together as one man into the street that was before the water gate; and they spake unto Ezra the scribe to bring the book of the law of Moses, which the Lord had commanded to Israel.

And Ezra, the priest, brought the law before the congregation both of men and women, and all that could hear with understanding, upon the first day of the seventh month.

*And he read therein before the street that was before the water gate **from the morning until midday**, before the men and the women, and those that could understand; **and the ears of all the people were attentive unto the book of the law.***

*And Ezra the scribe stood upon **a pulpit** of wood, which they had made for the purpose; and beside him stood*

*Mattithiah, and Shema, and Anaiah, and Urijah, and
Hilkiah, and Maaseiah, on his right hand; and on his
left hand, Pedaiah, and Mishael, and Malchiah, and
Hashum, and Hashbadana, Zechariah, and Meshullam.*

*And Ezra opened the book in the sight of all the
people (for he was above all the people); and **when
he opened it, all the people stood up:***

*And Ezra blessed the Lord, the great God. And all
the people answered, "Amen, Amen," with lifting
up their hands: and they bowed their heads and
worshipped the Lord with their faces to the ground.*

*Also Jeshua, and Bani, and Sherebiah, Jamin, Akkub,
Shabbethai, Hodijah, Maaseiah, Kelita, Azariah, Jozabad,
Hanan, Pelaiah, and the Levites, **caused the people to
understand the law: and the people stood in their place.***

***So they read in the book in the law of God
distinctly, and gave the sense, and caused
them to understand the reading.***

Some significant points in this passage should be emphasized.

1. Notice how long the sermon lasted. Not twenty minutes or
    forty minutes or even an hour, but from morning until mid-
    day. That means at least three hours. From all indications,
    they stood the entire time. Shame on those who watch the
    clock on Sundays while the minister preaches his heart out.
2. The congregation gave complete attention to what was
    being read from God's Book. They were diligent to listen
    and to contemplate the depth of what they were hearing.

(Romans 10:17: "So then faith cometh by hearing, and hearing by the word of God.")

3. Ezra preached from a *pulpit*. It had been made for that specific purpose. It put the preacher above everyone that they might see and, in a symbolic manner, they were looking up toward Heaven.

4. When the book of the law was read, the people gave it an extreme place of honor and respect by standing up. Standing before the Lord shows a deep sense of reverence. (Psalms 33:8: "Let all the earth fear the Lord: let all the inhabitants of the world stand in awe of him.")

5. As the book was read, clarification was given to help the listener gain increased understanding of the meaning. Significant principles were explained, and correct interpretations were given. (2 Peter 1:20: "Knowing this first, that no prophecy of the scripture is of any private interpretation.")

The importance of a God-sent message delivered by a faithful preacher to a listening congregation cannot be overstated. The very words of the minister's mouth are attended by the Holy Spirit. Serious issues are preached, and sober attitudes reflect on the weighty topics delivered. God, by His Spirit, pricks the listening hearts. Those who have ears to hear what the Spirit says to the churches are engrafted into the image of God's dear Son. The message of salvation is of grave importance to those who have not received the blessing of being born again. It has life and death consequences to the ones who have not yet believed.

The seriousness of what is going on spiritually in the Sunday sermon cannot be emphasized enough. That truth alone should motivate all Christians to attend each service, ready to pray and ask The Holy Spirit's power to convict lost sinners and strengthen weaker Christians in their faith. How is it that we can be so complacent? Satan has won another battle when we say we are too tired to get up for church. *If what you are doing on Saturday night keeps you from doing what you should be doing on Sunday morning, then you need to quit what you are doing on Saturday night!* Have we forgotten? Souls are at stake.

Most sermons last twenty to forty minutes. In that short period, the Lord must use His preachers to encourage the brokenhearted and clear away misconceptions of the hearers that they might plainly understand the truth. Hearts need to be convicted and forgiveness must be offered. Hope in the face of trials and tribulations must be authentic. Sin must be defined and abhorred. Sinners must be called to repent and be saved. Weak Christians need to be encouraged. That is a tall order for a twenty-minute sermon! If we have not come to His house to worship and take seriously that which is going on, then our hearts are far from Him. He deserves the Kiss of Adoration.

Everything done by the church throughout the week should be focused toward the Sunday sermon. Every visitation made, every prayer group, every Bible study, every Sunday school class should be funneling efforts toward bringing everyone to hear the Sunday message. The work that God does during the preaching of His Word goes unhindered when there is an atmosphere of religious reverence. The Bible declares that the law of the Lord is perfect, converting the soul (Psalm 19:7). In the correct worship atmosphere, demons flee because the gates of hell cannot prevail against the church. It is high time that we put the "How-To" sermons on hold and get back to preaching the clear choice between fire and brimstone or mansions and streets of gold. The world desperately needs it, and those in the world are dying without it. Grace is still being extended, but the time for mercy is running out.

These Scriptures need to be repeated as we end this chapter: Romans 10:14: "How then shall they call on him in whom they have not believed? And how shall they believe in him of whom they have not heard? And how shall they hear without a preacher?"

Chapter Eight
THE HEATHEN

*For from the rising of the sun even unto the going
down of the same my name shall be great among
the Gentiles; and in every place incense shall
be offered unto my name, and a pure offering:*
**for my name shall be great among the hea-
then, saith the Lord of hosts** *(Malachi 1:11).*

Psalms chapter two starts with a question: "Why do the heathen rage?" What a great question! We have a God who loves us, died for us, and offers salvation to us. You would think the Lord would be embraced. So why all the animosity? The hatred of God that exists seems to border on excessive hysteria. People rant, they rave, and the psalm says they imagine a vain thing. Whatever their reasons, it is undoubtedly a vain thing to stand against The Almighty. Wicked men always feel God's rule and His Law are too binding and too restricting. In truth, His commands keep us from harm. The flagman on the road warns of danger ahead. His instructions are sometimes to stop, sometimes to proceed with caution, and sometimes to turn around and travel another way. But the heathen wants to go his own way. Proverbs 14:12: "There is a way which seemeth right unto a man, but the end thereof are the ways of death."

The word *heathen* gives us some insight into the character of those who fit this description. *Strong's Concordance* defines the word as "a troop of animals." That sounds like a good description. After all, the Bible says they are brute beasts. Jude 10: "But these speak evil of those things which they know not: but what they know naturally, *as brute beasts*, in those things they corrupt themselves." They want to be allowed to continue to do what comes naturally as animals, and they shun the spiritual things that are the gift of God. This is a vivid example of two kingdoms. One is a kingdom of light, one is a kingdom of darkness, and darkness can't stand the light. Proverbs 4:19: "The way of the wicked is as darkness: they know not at what they stumble."

The heathen's rage is deliberate. They take counsel together to see how they can bring down the kingdom of light. They remove the Ten Commandments from the walls of schools; they take Bibles out of classrooms; they block Christian youth from having after-school Bible clubs; they cease prayer at the flag; they legalize abortion; they champion homosexuality; and the list goes on and on. Rest assured, however, wisdom on all these issues will trump the foolishness of their dark kingdom. Ecclesiastes 2:13: "Then I saw that wisdom excelleth folly, as far as light excelleth darkness." It is no wonder that the Lord stands ready to exhibit His wrath. David, the little shepherd boy, slew Goliath. The heathens in this world have forgotten they are provoking the Great Shepherd! *Kiss the Son. He is the One who is about to get angry. His wrath is kindling as we speak.*

DARKNESS AND LIGHT

Every Christian remembers walking in the kingdom of darkness before their salvation. They praise God that they have seen the light and they pray to God that those in darkness will also see the light. Why? Because it is after you are saved that the reality of the hell you just missed starts to sink in. Jesus said that He is the light of the world. He is a great light. His light shines on all who have called upon the Lord to be saved. All God's children sing His praises knowing they have been passed from death unto life. Isaiah 9:2: "The people that walked in darkness have seen a great light: they that dwell in the land of the shadow of death, upon them hath the light shined." The Lord Jesus pardons those who believe and He stands ready to punish those who do not. The heathen thinks he is morally good enough and that he is the one who is tolerant and loving. He sees the Christian as judgmental. He believes that Christians are the intolerant and hateful group.

Let the warning be clear. Let the line be drawn in plain sight for all to see.

Isaiah 5:20: "Woe unto them that call evil good, and good evil; that put darkness for light, and light for darkness; that put bitter for sweet, and sweet for bitter!" Each person must make a choice to kiss the *Son*.

The heathen cannot stand the warnings. They would rather hear about God's love and how long He will be patient with their rebellion. They love the sermons on His grace and mercy but when—or, if—His righteous indignation and holiness and justice are pointed out, they rage, "My God is not like that." Let it be stated explicitly: *Their god is "not like that" because their god is not the God of the Bible.* Their god is a fairy-tale god that makes them feel better about themselves.

Anyone who names the name of the Lord should have a healthy dose of fear and trembling. As we live day to day with the gift of salvation that the Lord has given to those who are saved, we are to carefully handle that salvation in fear and trembling. Philippians 2:12: "Wherefore, my beloved, as ye have always obeyed, not as in my presence only, but now much more in my absence, work out your own salvation *with fear and trembling*." Most of the teaching in today's churches equate fear with reverence and awe, but how many Christians really connect the dots to *trembling*? The Greek word for trembling is *tromos*, and it means quaking with fear. Let's remember that Jesus said we are to fear the One who has the power to cast us into hell. Matthew 10:28: "And fear not them which kill the body but are not able to kill the soul: but rather fear him which is able to destroy both soul and body in hell."

Let the heathen rage. It doesn't change a thing. The outcome is already set. Jesus is King of all kings. One day soon, the prayer "thy kingdom come, thy will be done, here on earth as it is in heaven" will be answered. And when it is, the heathen will be nowhere around. They will be banished. They will be gone. They will have begun their tortuous eternity. Psalms 10:16: "The Lord is King for ever and ever: the *heathen* are perished out of his land."

With just a word from Jesus, the kingdoms of this world will become the kingdoms of the King. With the same vocal authority He used in Genesis chapter one, He will melt this earth into a cauldron of fire and brimstone. Psalms 46:6: "The *heathen* raged, the kingdoms were moved: he uttered his voice, the earth melted." In that day it will matter not what the heathen says. He or she will be utterly lost. The wrath of God, which no one wants to hear about, will be directed at them. Psalms 79:6: "Pour out thy wrath upon the *heathen* that have not known thee, and upon the kingdoms that have not called upon thy name."

The heathen get their bravado from the fact they have not received any "biblical retribution" when they have sinned. So they continue to rage: "Where is this God?" Psalms 79:10: "Wherefore should the *heathen* say, 'Where is their God?' Let him be known among the heathen in our sight by the revenging of the blood of thy servants which is shed." The Bible says that God does not forget the cry of the humble. Neither does He forget the rage of the heathen. Yet, the heathen go right on sinning. And the pit they are digging for themselves gets deeper and deeper. Psalms 9:15: "The *heathen are sunk down in the pit that they made*: in the net which they hid is their own foot taken."

Instead of raging, the heathen should be falling down in humble adoration and meek thanksgiving that the punishment he or she rightfully deserves has once again been tempered by the longsuffering of God. God the Father is ready to hand over the reins of His terror to His Son Jesus, whenever the Lord finally asks. Psalms 2:8: "Ask of me, and I shall give thee the *heathen* for thine inheritance, and the uttermost parts of the earth for thy possession." Rest assured, Jesus will ask someday because all judgment has been given into His hands to be administered at the appointed time.

Some still try to believe that there will be no personal payment for their sins. A sermon preached with apocalyptic images of a world steeped in war and dripping with dead bodies seems, to the heathen, to be only a manipulation tactic employed by some hardhearted preacher. This could not be further from the truth. Preachers are under strict orders from the King to issue the warnings He has declared. And those same preachers have the blessed message that there is a way out of the coming doom to those who would believe and trust in what Jesus Christ did for them at the cross. But the heathen rage and try to write their preferred end to their story. Listen to the warning carefully: Psalms 110:6: "He shall *judge among the heathen, he shall fill the places with the dead bodies;* he shall wound the heads over many countries."

Hear the question again: Psalms 115:2: "Wherefore should the heathen say, 'Where is now their God?'" The answer is that He is everywhere. He is omnipresent. He is standing at the door of a repentant sinner's heart while, at the same time, He is mounting His white horse as He prepares to enter battle. Jesus will not be riding that horse for show. He will be coming to tread the winepress of the wrath of Almighty God. Revelation 19:11: "And I saw Heaven opened, and behold a white horse, and he that sat upon him was called Faithful and True, and in righteousness, *he doth judge and make war.*" Heathen beware. He is coming for you. He came two thousand years ago in love. He is coming back in judgment.

The heathen believes none of this and spends his or her life trying to build a name for themselves. They do it in the entertainment business. They establish some measure of notoriety to their name only to die premature deaths from overdoses, alcoholism, suicide, or sexually transmitted diseases. Those left in their industry try to keep alive the name of the one who has died, as if that will bring some solace to all involved. How tragic all this is. When Jesus comes to judge, He will even do away with their names. Psalms 9:5: "Thou hast rebuked the *heathen*, thou hast destroyed the wicked, *thou hast put out their name for ever and ever.*" All the effort that people expend to "make a name" for themselves will have been utterly useless. And to think that they could have had a new name written in glory.

Who Are the Heathen?

The image of Jesus ready to mount the horse He will ride to judgment may seem like an extravagant exaggeration to some. The heathen does not believe that judgment will come at all. *In fact, the heathen do not think they are the heathen.* After all, when is the last time that you heard the word *heathen* used in a sermon? The word is almost antiquated. Most people today would define heathen as some remote tribe found in the Amazon regions. The word would certainly not apply to the "good people" in America today. Listen, dear reader: the heathen is anyone and everyone who rebels against the only true God of the universe. His judgment is near. Jesus' foot may well be in the stirrup. Ezekiel 30:3: "For the day is *near*, even the day of the Lord is *near*, a cloudy day; it shall be the time of the *heathen*."

In the Old Testament, the heathen were all the other nations apart from Israel. The symbolism is that the heathen are those outside of God's kingdom. Today, we all fall into the category of the heathen before we yield our heart to the Lord. The heathen is opposed to God. Whether openly or secretly, their hearts are far from Him. All those outside of God's kingdom are digging a hole for themselves. Every day that hole gets deeper and deeper. The Bible is clear that it is their own doing. Psalms 9:15: "*The heathen* is sunk down in the pit that they made: in the net which they hid is their own foot taken."

It is not too late to ask the Lord to save. It does not matter how deep the pit has gotten in one's life. The Lord can rescue anyone from the depths of the deepest pit if they will call out to Him. The simplest prayer we can pray is "Help!" It is a prayer that says from the heart that I know the trouble I am in, and I need deliverance. The word *help* contains within its cry the realization that the Lord is the only one who can save us. It is an admission that by our spirit we need to be saved. Psalms 40:2, 3: "He brought me up also out of an horrible pit, out of the miry clay, and set my feet upon a rock, and established my goings. And he hath put a new song in my mouth, even praise unto our God: many shall see it, and fear, and shall trust in the Lord."

Without the soul's recognition of its need for salvation, and with no call for help, the only thing left for the heathen is judgment. Psalms 9:19: "Arise, O Lord; let not man prevail: let the heathen be judged in thy sight." Please hear the truth. Wrath is coming. Anger is coming. Vengeance is coming. Punishments are soon to be administered by the hand of God and by the sword of the Son. The day of the Lord will be vast and extensive, sweeping over the entire world. It will not miss anyone but will encompass all heathen. The Lord takes pleasure in His people, but He will not pity the heathen. He is coming. Psalms 149:7-9: "To *execute vengeance* upon *the heathen*, and *punishments* upon the people."

Repent! Repent! Repent! Before it is too late . . . *Repent!* Don't listen to the lies of the adversary. Do not hearken to the dishonesties of the deceiver. Give not heed to the lures of the devil. He is a liar and the father of lies. He still lies. He will always lie because there is no truth in him. He wanted to be God, but he will never be God. Satan is the original heathen! Jeremiah 10:2: "Thus saith the Lord: Learn not the way of the *heathen.*"

The temptation that the heathen fall to is to try to be their own God. The attraction to rule one's life is as old as the garden of Eden.

Satan told Eve, in Genesis 3:5: "For God doth know that in the day ye eat thereof, then your eyes shall be opened, *and ye shall be as gods, knowing good and evil.*" This generation thinks, more than ever, that it will be the one to accomplish godhood.

There are unprecedented advancements in science today. There are entirely new areas of research and discovery that have never existed before. Scientists have begun genetically manipulating animals to create a better food source for humans. Modern breeds of livestock have dramatic differences from their ancestors as a result of breeding strategies. For example, milk production per cow has increased among dairy cattle. Similarly, breeding programs have resulted in lean, fast-growing pigs. Chickens from recent experimentation each produce more than 250 eggs per year—approximately double that produced in 1950—again mainly due to genetic selection. The underlying goal in all this is to find a way for man to live forever. It makes no difference how much the world advances and consults together with its science. In the non-God approach to immortality, the heathen fulfills the Scriptures without knowing it. Psalms 33:10: "The Lord bringeth the counsel of the heathen to nought: *he maketh the devices of the people of none effect.*" No matter how hard or how long they try, immortality will not be found apart from God.

The Bible states that the wages of sin is death. Eternal life cannot happen where there is sin. If we could live forever in sin, the depravity would be unimaginable. Scripture states that the final victory will be a victory over death and it will be the Lord's victory. 1 Corinthians 15:53, 54: "For this corruptible must put on incorruption, and this mortal must put on immortality; So when this corruptible shall have put on incorruption, and this mortal shall have put on immortality, then shall be brought to pass the saying that is written, *Death is swallowed up in victory.*"

It will not matter if science can give us the sense of smell of a dog or the eyesight of an eagle, the fact remains that we will live in our sins and, apart from salvation in Jesus Christ, we will die in our sins.

It is not that the heathen did not know there was a God. They have heard Him preached. Every generation hears the message of salvation. They may not listen. They may not believe. They may deny there is a God. But they have heard it proclaimed. God makes sure of that so that none will have an excuse. Psalms 98:2: "The Lord *hath made known his salvation*: his righteousness hath he openly shewed in the sight of the *heathen*."

When the heathen are judged at the end of time, there will be no joy. There was no joy at Calvary when our sins were judged on the cross. The cross was the first judgment on sin. The end of time will be the final judgment on sin. The heathen, in his final sentence, will forever abhor the fact that he raged against the first judgment. There was no joy when Jesus died on the cross. But there would be joy to all those who would call upon His name to be saved. Jesus saw that day, and it brought Him immense joy. Hebrews 12:2: "Looking unto Jesus the author and finisher of our faith; *who for the joy that was set before him endured the cross,* despising the shame, and is set down at the right hand of the throne of God."

Oh, dear heathen, do not rage against Him but repent to Him. Do not curse Him but call upon Him. Do not hate Him but hold tight to Him. He is the King of Kings. He is the Lord of Lords. He is worthy to be praised. He is the Mighty God, the Prince of Peace, the Everlasting Father. He is Wonderful and Magnificent and Holy and True. There are no gods before Him, and there will be no gods after Him. Psalms 95:3: "For the Lord is a great God and a great King above all gods." He is God to the saint, and He is God over the sinner. Stop raging, you hardhearted. Be silent and hear while you may. Jesus is going to make the kingdoms of this world His own. He says to those who have not yet understood (Psalms 46:10): "Be still, and know that I am God: I will be exalted among the *heathen*, I will be exalted in the earth."

The heathen has profaned the name of the Lord down through the generations of humanity. The third commandment given to Moses is found in Ex. 20:7: "Thou shalt not take the name of the Lord thy God in vain; for the Lord will not hold him guiltless that taketh his name in vain." If they ever needed proof as to who the real God is, all they have to do is listen to what name is always taken in vain by the heathen of today. Is it Buddha? Is it Mohammed? Is it Krishna? Is it Allah or Absolute Consciousness or Mother Universe? What is the name used in vain over and over again in movies, on television, at ball games, on the street, and in music? The obvious answer is: Jesus. The name of Jesus is the only name that breaks the third commandment. The magnificent name of Jesus is spewed and soiled and profaned without any regard for that third commandment. The Lord says: don't do it. And He goes on to say that anyone who does will not be held guiltless.

If any of the other names were used in vain, they might think they have reason to wonder who the Lord is. But the truth is, none of the other names are ever used in a profane way. It is the name of Jesus that is dragged through gutters of filthy language a thousand times a thousand times a day. They will be declared guilty for the vain use of that marvelous name: Ezekiel 36:23: "And I will sanctify my great name, which was profaned among the *heathen*, which ye have profaned in the midst of them; and the *heathen* shall know that I am the Lord, saith the Lord God, when I shall be sanctified in you before their eyes."

The Lord's name is above every name. His name will be raised and exalted soon. Everyone will reverence His name some day. Philippians 2:9-11: "Wherefore God also hath highly exalted him, and given him a name which is above every name: That at the name of Jesus every knee should bow, of things in heaven, and things in earth, and things under the earth; And that every tongue should confess that Jesus Christ is Lord, to the glory of God the Father."

Ezekiel 39:7: "So will I make my *holy name* known in the midst of my people Israel; and *I will not let them pollute my holy name any more*: and *the heathen* shall know that I am the Lord, the Holy One in Israel."

Take note, dear reader: *there is still time to repent.*

CHAPTER NINE
THE WICKED

*"Thou hast rebuked the **heathen,** thou hast de-stroyed **the wicked,** thou hast put out their name for ever and ever"* (Psalms 9:5).

The Bible describes the heathen as those who are not of God's people. Sometimes as individuals and sometimes as nations. In many cases, they are openly rebellious against God and His church. Within the category of the heathen, there exists an especially offensive class of sinners the Lord refers to as the wicked. The Scriptures have much to say about this appalling group. The curse of God is upon them. Proverbs 3:33: "The curse of the Lord is in the house of the wicked: but he blesseth the habitation of the just." We are about to discover, in this chapter, that God has a real disdain for those He calls the wicked. Does this mean that a wicked person can never be saved? Absolutely not! There is no unforgivable sin except the rejection of the Lord's offer of salvation. The grace and mercy that the Lord offers does not exclude any group of people. God will actively bless the homes of righteous people. But, just as assuredly, He will actively curse the house of the wicked. We will leave the interpretation of when and how He does that to Him, but, at the very least, it means that He withdraws any of His heavenly advantages.

There was a time in the history of the preached word in which the word *heathen* appeared in the messages of caution. God's concern was that all men, everywhere, would hear the clear warnings from Him. It is the preacher's responsibility to make clear what it is that God hates and to pronounce the penalties that will befall them if they choose their own way. In Scripture, the category of sinners that the Lord calls "the wicked" has proceeded a long way down their path to damnation.

The Lord sees this group as evil men. He warns against any participation with them in their evil ways. Proverbs 4:14, 15: "Enter not into the path of *the wicked*, and go not in the way of evil men. Avoid it, pass not by it, turn from it, and pass away." We are to keep clear of the things the wicked might do. We are to withdraw from any activity that is an obvious abomination to our God. The Lord detests wickedness. He denounces it throughout His Word.

Who are the wicked? They are the pornographers. They are the human traffickers. They are the drug dealers, the rapists, the mass murderers, and child molesters. This does not exhaust the list, but you get the idea. And it needs to be taken further. Wicked people are involved in anything that God calls an abomination. For every pornographer, there are millions who rent and buy the filth. For every person who sells women and children for sex, there are countless millions of wicked men and women who pay for the opportunity to indulge their lusts. When it comes to pornography, we should listen to the psalmist, who said:

> "I will set **no wicked** thing before mine eyes: I hate
> the work of them that turn aside; it shall not cleave
> to me. A froward heart shall depart from me: I will
> not know a wicked person" (Psalms 101:3, 4).

We are to hate what God hates. We are to abhor what God abhors. We are to preach against sin, warn of its consequences, and offer salvation as the alternative. God is still showing patience. How much longer will He wait? He can save and will save anyone willing to repent. But time is running out.

There are "good" people who do not do the wicked things in this world, but apart from being born again, they are just as lost the class called the wicked. The Pharisees did all the right things on the outside, but Jesus said that, inside, they were full of dead men's bones. Unsaved wicked people need to repent. Unsaved "good" people need to repent.

To repent means to turn around and go in another direction. It is a wicked heart becoming a soft heart as it calls on the Lord to be saved. To continue down the road of destruction is madness. Proverbs 4:19: "The way of *the wicked* is as darkness: they know not at what they stumble."

WICKED HEARTS

The Lord describes our hearts as He sees them. Jeremiah 17:9: "The heart is deceitful above all things, and desperately *wicked*: who can know it?" The lost world does not believe their hearts are wicked because people are being deceived by the great deceiver. The heart is not just wicked (which is bad enough) but it is *desperately* wicked. Without Christ, our hearts are perilously vicious and evil. *Desperate* gives the connotation of hopelessness. Apart from Jesus Christ, all is lost. All is hopeless. A desperately wicked heart is almost beyond hope. A desperately wicked heart has sunk dangerously close to surrender. The way God sees it, the desperately wicked heart of a soul sold out to sin is of very little value. (Proverbs 10:20: "The heart of the wicked is of little worth.") The Lord has very little regard for this heart. It would be insignificant to Him except that He loves His creation. We should give even more importance to the verse that says, in Romans 5:8: "But God commendeth his love toward us, in that, while we were yet sinners, Christ died for us." Here is a humbling statement. The God of all creation suffered an excruciating death for worthless hearts. We are the objects of that love, and we should treasure that fact. The consequence of ignoring His love will be vicious and unrelenting.

It is no wonder that we are urged not to even touch the unclean things of this world. Wicked men prepare and produce every manner of a vile device for the consumption of a lust-filled humanity. We are not to be drawn away to the evil things of iniquity. Psalms 141:4: "Incline not my heart to any evil thing, to practise *wicked* works with men that work iniquity: and let me not eat of their dainties." God says withdraw yourself. Satan says indulge yourself. God says flee youthful lusts. Satan says fulfill those youthful lusts.

With the advent of technology, the wizards of wickedness have sunken to new lows in their depravity. Human trafficking has become a worldwide epidemic. The marketing of little girls and boys just to fulfill the temporary lusts of a depraved mind is atrocious. Those who sell children are *wicked*. Those who pay money to rape and abuse these little ones are detestable.

The film industry continues to package the offensive and corrupt sin nature of man. Actors portray the vilest behavior the human heart can contrive. Those in Hollywood brag of their wickedness. They sponsor awards shows to gloat upon themselves. They exalt the most depraved of men and women. Psalms 10:3: "For the wicked boasteth of his heart's desire, and blesseth the covetous, whom the Lord abhorreth." The Internet pours out pornography to millions of desktops all over the world. God hates those who are involved in these sins. Part of the sinner's ability to rationalize his sins is wrapped up in his wrongful perception of God. It may be hard for the mind that has been mesmerized by most of the preaching of the twenty-first century. All he has heard is that God is love. For us to say that God hates an individual that is wicked is a strong statement. But it is only repeating what the

Lord has said Himself. Psalms 11:5: "The Lord trieth the righteous: but *the wicked* and him that loveth violence his soul *hateth.*"

One of the seven things God hates the most is a heart that devises wicked imaginations. The sheer magnitude of the wickedness produced and purchased today is staggering and must have the Lord ready to blow the judgment trumpet. Christians should offer up the prayer of the psalmist in Psalm 140:8: "Grant not, O Lord, the desires of *the wicked*: further not *his wicked* device; lest they exalt themselves."

The wicked are headed for judgment. It may be their own fleshly desires that are their undoing. Proverbs 5:22: "His own iniquities shall take *the wicked* himself, and he shall be holden with the cords of his sins." The chains are strong that bind them to their wicked ways. The cords are tied tight to their sins. Only a cry of desperation and repentance and a prayer for forgiveness stands between them and an unspeakable eternity of torment. If they do not call upon the Lord, they will be damned. How many have died from AIDS? How many have perished from dirty needles? Whether intentionally or not, how many have overdosed on drugs or drank themselves, literally, to death? They are killed by the very sins they worship. How much longer do we believe the Lord is going to wait? His patience is drawing to a close. He will soon do away with the wicked. Psalms 139:19: "Surely, thou wilt slay *the wicked*, O God: depart from me therefore, ye bloody men." Hear the choice again: Palms 145:20: "The Lord preserveth all them that love him: but all *the wicked* will he destroy."

One of the reasons God hates the wicked and his wickedness is because of their hatred of the righteous. Those who are saved and have been given the righteousness that is in Christ are the apple of God's eye. Our prayer to God is found in Psalms 17:8, 9: "Keep me as the *apple of the eye*, hide me under the shadow of thy wings, From *the wicked* that oppress me, from my deadly enemies, who compass me about." Satan schemes are to surround us with the filthy temptations of his kingdom. He attacks us when we have been away from the

Word of God for a while and are spiritually famished. The devil waits until we are tired and irritable to assault us. Thank God that it is the Lord who keeps us and protects us.

An eternity in hell awaits those who will not repent. Psalms 9:17: *"The wicked shall be turned into hell."* This truth should give pause to all who are lost. They need to come to their senses. They are in desperate trouble. They lift themselves up. They pat themselves on the backs. They look down their noses at the Christians who humbly serve the Lord. They imagine themselves great. But the truth is that the least in the kingdom of heaven will be far, far better off than the greatest in hell.

The Truth

Wicked men loathe this truth. They pretend to have life, and they go their own way, but they are full of dead men's bones. Their way is a way that leads to their destruction. God will banish them to an eternal fire where they will rot forever. These are His words. Proverbs 10:7: "The memory of the just is blessed: but the name of *the wicked* shall rot." The wicked believe everything that is opposed to God. They listen to "their father" (those are Jesus' words): the devil. He is the father of lies. Satan offers them many ways. Jesus says, "I am the way." Satan confuses the truth. Jesus says, "I am the truth." Satan tempts them to live it up in life. Jesus says, "I am the life." Satan says, "Don't worry. There are many ways to Heaven." Jesus says, "No man comes to the Father but by Me."

Remember that the Bible says that there are none who are righteous, "no not one." The scriptures are clear that all we like sheep have gone astray. Lost people who fall into the category that the world would call "good people" are experts at fooling themselves. They think they are virtuous. Or, at the very least, they think they are good enough. They measure their lives against others. They see themselves as better than most. Their self-appraisal has them convinced that they are alright.

There is only one evaluation that God accepts. He holds us up to the mirror of Jesus Christ's perfection. To that end, we all fall short. But they are misled, and in turn they deceive others. The wicked can look good on the outside. They can be outwardly charming, but inside they are rotten. Psalms 5:9: "For there is no faithfulness in their mouth; their inward part is very *wickedness*; their throat is an open sepulchre; they flatter with their tongue."

The evil nature of the wicked starts at an early age. The psalmist has this to say, in Psalms 58:3: "*The wicked* are estranged from the womb: they go astray *as soon as they be born*, speaking lies." What the psalmist means is that those who eventually become "the wicked," show, for the most part, even from their early childhood, a strong tendency towards evil. The most innocent of babies born have within themselves the seeds of wickedness that fan the flames of hell. Proverbs 20:11: "Even a child is known by his doings, whether his work be pure, and whether it be right." But just because we are born with more of a tendency toward evil than an inclination toward righteousness, this does not mean we can avoid our responsibility. The wicked harden themselves against the grace of God and close their ears against His Word. They build themselves up in wickedness. Without knowing it, they are preparing themselves for a horrible end. Without salvation their ruin is inevitable. It is not merely that the predisposition to wickedness has developed itself, but it has advanced unchecked.

Wicked people cultivate their wickedness. They make sure there are no obstructions to their quest for more extreme fleshly satisfaction. Any influences that may attempt to arrest their insatiable desires they resist and reject. Jesus was right when He said: "Ye do always resist the Holy Ghost." The things that were at first tendencies in their behavior give way to unrelenting addictions.

Maybe the woeful part of all of this is that the wicked deny reality. The drug user wants more drugs. He can never get enough. The serial killer kills again and again because it is never enough. The sexual perversions of many create a lifestyle that goes unchecked. Their thirst for more and more persists because of an overwhelming, overpowering urge that can only be temporarily satisfied. But they deny the truth. Their only hope is in the Lord. Jesus said that our thirst can be fulfilled. John 4:13, 14: "Jesus answered and said unto her, 'Whosoever drinketh of this water shall thirst again, But whosoever drinketh of the water that I shall give him shall never thirst, but the water that I shall give him shall be in him a well of water springing up into everlasting life.'"

LOSS OF CONSCIENCE

One of the greatest dangers to someone wicked is the loss of their conscience. Once that happens, there is no more hope. Not everyone has a chance at a deathbed confession. Romans 1:28: "And even as they did not like to retain God in their knowledge, God gave them over to a reprobate mind, to do those things which are not convenient." Let's put it another way. There is a point of no return with God, and it does not always come at the time of death. That point in life comes when there is no more struggle from within a person against sin and evil. Rather than fight corruption, they delight in it. It makes no difference what grace is shown to them. The influences of righteousness around them matter no more. They are on a one-way ticket to hell. The prophet Isaiah said it this way (26:10): "Let favour be shewed to *the wicked, yet will he not learn righteousness*: in the land of uprightness will he deal unjustly, and will not behold the majesty of the Lord."

The power of the wicked will be destroyed someday. His plans shall be defeated at the coming of the Lord. We who have loved the Lord and have had to see the ruin of lives because of wickedness will finally rejoice. Vengeance is mine, says the Lord. Those who have loved Him will be there that day to witness Him exact His judgment. Psalms 58:10, 11: "*The righteous shall rejoice when he seeth the vengeance*: he shall wash his feet in the blood of *the wicked*. So that a man shall say, Verily there is a reward for the righteous: verily he is a God that judgeth in the earth."

The wicked only have expectations in this life. They fill their years with all the lusts of the flesh they can achieve. But they are running out of years. Proverbs 10:27, 28: "The fear of the LORD pro-longeth days: *but the years of the wicked shall be shortened.* The hope of the righteous shall be gladness: but *the expectation of the wicked shall perish.*" The lives of the wicked are in a temporary time-out from hell.

MEPHIBOSHETH

There is a fascinating character found in the Bible by the name of Mephibosheth. His story is found in Second Samuel, chapters four through twenty-one. Mephibosheth was the son of Jonathan, David's close friend. Mephibosheth was only five years old when both his father and his grandfather Saul were killed. In a hurry to escape the feared Philistines, the nurse grabbed the little boy to flee, and he fell, leaving his two feet crippled.

Later in the story, David realizes that Mephibosheth is alive. He summons him to live in the palace with the king, where he ate at the table of the king continuously. 2 Samuel 9:7, 8: "And David said unto him, 'Fear not: for I will surely shew thee kindness for Jonathan thy father's sake, and will restore thee all the land of Saul, thy father; and thou shalt eat bread at my table continually.' And he bowed himself, and said, 'What is thy servant, that thou shouldest look upon such a dead dog as I am?'" Imagine the picture that is drawn here. Every evening, Mephibosheth was invited to eat at the table of King David. A typical dinner with the king would be filled with guests that would include princes and governors and judges and other dignitaries. To have a crippled man at the king's table would generally seem odd and out of place. We should not overlook this precious symbolism. We who are like Mephibosheth have been crippled by the wickedness of sin. Rather than the Lord shunning us, He bids us to live with Him in His palace and offers us a seat at His table.

We too are no better than "a dead dog." Dogs are looked down upon in many societies. We have sayings within our culture that reflect a negative attitude toward dogs. We say things like "he has gone to the dogs" or "if you lay down with dogs, you will get up with fleas." Once a lost soul realizes his appalling nature there is no more room for pretending there is any good thing in him. We are like a dead dog that lies in the dust of its wickedness. The miracle is that the Son of God sees us in that state and is willing to share His domain with us if we will call upon Him. It matters not to Him how much we have been crippled by our sin. A dog that is shown a little kindness will love its master and be faithful to Him all the days of its life. How much more should we who are saved do the same? Jesus put it this way (John 14:2, 3): "In my Father's house are many mansions: if it were not so, I would have told you. I go to prepare a place for you. And if I go and prepare a place for you, I will come again, and receive you unto myself; that where I am, there ye may be also." This is His invitation to live with Him in His palace. Many who are wicked still refuse the offer. They refuse His way. Countless sinners still choose the way of Judas. They are filled with the hatred of Cain, who was the first murderer in Scripture. Like Pilate, they try to wash away any responsibility for their actions. But their hands remain bloodstained and guilty.

Today, we pray for all those caught up in evil. It is not for us to judge when the Lord will erase their names from the Book of Life. Only He knows when they have crossed the line from hope to hopelessness. The fact that evil men are still alive shows the mercy and patience of God because judgment has not yet been meted out to them. But judgment will come. God will accomplish His will in due time. The wicked need to beware!

Perhaps a scriptural reminder is in order:

1. Proverbs 10:28 . . . . . *"the expectation of the wicked shall perish."*
2. Proverbs 11:5 . . . . . *"the wicked shall fall by his own wickedness."*
3. Proverbs 11:10 . . . . *"when the wicked perish, there is shouting."*

4. Proverbs 11:21 . . . . *"the wicked shall not be unpunished."*
5. Proverbs 11:23 . . . . *"the expectation of the wicked is wrath."*

The wicked can expect wrath. He can only expect wrath. And he will receive that wrath for all eternity. That should give us even more reason to pause and wonder at the depth of God's love. He knows who we are and what we are, but He still chose to offer His love to us through His Son Jesus. A wicked person can be saved if he will turn from his wickedness and turn to the Lord.

CHAPTER 10

WICKEDNESS

*"As saith the proverb of the ancients, **wickedness** proceedeth from **the wicked** . . . ." (1 Samuel 24:13).*

Wickedness is wrapped in the very essence of our being. Wickedness is the potential to act out the extremes of our sin nature. The Bible says that it is in us from the days of our youth. Wickedness is not only a part of us, it reigns in us. It controls us. Our thoughts and the intents of our heart are evil. The psalmist says that our sins are more than the hairs on our head. Psalms 40:12: "For innumerable evils have compassed me about: mine iniquities have taken hold upon me, so that I am not able to look up; they are more than the hairs of mine head: therefore my heart faileth me." Without a cure for this condition, we will receive an eternal death. Like anyone in a desperate situation, we should cry out for help. Psalms 40:13: "Be pleased, O Lord, to deliver me: O Lord, make haste to help me."

The Lord loves righteousness with the same intensity that He hates wickedness. The cross was love, and the cross was wrath. It was love because He loved us and did not want us to perish under the consequences of our sins. It was wrath because God hated iniquity and God required punishment for sin. He took our wickedness upon himself and nailed our sins to the cross. He buried iniquities in the grave. Jesus resurrected to tread the winepress of the wrath of Almighty God against wickedness. Jesus, who knew no sin, was made sin that we could become the righteousness of God and be delivered from our wickedness. In simple terms, the Lord took upon Himself the sins of the whole world—past, present, and future. Jesus has waited patiently for more than two thousand years to end the rebellion of all humanity. But when Jesus comes to judge, He will do away with all wickedness forever. That means that He will have to do away with the wicked.

There is an event coming that is commonly referred to as the Rapture of the church. This doctrine has been proven in hundreds of books and articles on the subject. It is not this author's intent to rehash the validity of the teaching on this great truth. In simple terms, it will be a moment of time, in the future, when God will instantly remove all true Christians from the face of the earth. Paul's letter to the church in Thessalonica describes it in detail (1 Thessalonians 4:16, 17): "For the Lord himself shall descend from heaven with a shout, with the voice of the archangel, and *with the trump of God*: and the dead in Christ shall rise first: Then we which are alive and remain shall be caught up together with them in the clouds, to meet the Lord in the air: and so shall we ever be with the Lord."

The only ones left behind will be the lost. Those who have never surrendered to the authority of the King of kings will be in for the shock of their lives. Without the restraining presence of the church preaching righteousness and the Holy Spirit's convicting power attending the message of salvation, the inhabitants of the earth will quickly perish. Isaiah 18:3: "*All ye inhabitants of the world, and dwellers on the earth, see ye when he lifteth up an ensign on the mountains; and when he bloweth a trumpet, hear ye.*" When the Lord blows His trumpet and removes the church, those who remain will be under the curse of God, and they will be left to suffer God's wrath upon the earth. Their chance to call upon Him has passed. They will now reap the results of their decision to reject and discard the Son of God. They have cast Him off, and they have abandoned Him just as He was treated on the day of His crucifixion.

The Lord will afflict them and plague them. He will trouble them and torment them. He will bring His reproach upon them and abolish them. Deuteronomy 28:20: "The Lord shall send upon thee *cursing, vexation, and rebuke,* in all that thou settest thine hand unto for to do, until thou be *destroyed,* and until *thou perish quickly*; because of *the wickedness* of thy doings, whereby thou hast forsaken me."

The damage that the Lord will execute will be irreversible. The devastation He will bring will touch every aspect of their lives. Deuteronomy 28:15-19: "All these curses shall come upon thee, and overtake thee: Cursed shalt thou be in the city, and cursed shalt thou be in the field. Cursed shall be thy basket and thy store. Cursed shall be the fruit of thy body, and the fruit of thy land, the increase of thy kine, and the flocks of thy sheep. Cursed shalt thou be when thou comest in, and cursed shalt thou be when thou goest out."

God will bring utter destruction upon them. After the church is gone, the savagery of mankind will be unleashed in this world. The evil hearts of men will run rampant. Every barbaric act that one man could commit against another will be done. Their vileness will be overwhelming. Their depraved imaginations will know no bounds. Left unchecked, the immorality of their evil hearts will be in a freefall of degeneration. This may sound shocking as you read these descriptions. You may ask "Why?" The psalmist gives us the answer (Psalm 5:9): "For there is no faithfulness in their mouth; *their inward part* is very *wickedness*; their throat is an open sepulchre; they flatter with their tongue."

The Lord will judge. He will not let sin go unpunished forever. It will be because it is His character and nature to condemn evil, and it will be in response to the prayer that the psalm writer taught us to pray in Psalms 7:9: "Oh let *the wickedness of the wicked come to an end . . .* " Very little is preached about this from our pulpits today.

What Is Wickedness?

Given the prophesied outcome of this vile world, it would be good for us to evaluate just what it is that God calls wickedness. Here are some examples.

> 1. **Pornography:** Leviticus 18:17: "Thou shalt not uncover the *nakedness* of a woman . . . . . it is *wickedness*."

We have had the problem of pornography from the beginning of time. Drawings on cave walls and artwork in Egyptian tombs bear this out. But never has porn been so prevalent and easily accessible as it is in our generation. With the advent of the Internet, the onslaught of the lust of the eyes has never been more intense. From the halls of Congress to the classrooms of junior high schools, we have seen the devastation that has been brought on by the new issue of "sexting." Congressmen have been shamed, and children have had their innocence robbed because of this digital devil. Teenagers are having their perceptions warped about love and intimacy within God's plan.

It is evident to any honest thinking person that pornography is not a victimless crime. Serial killers like Ted Bundy and Jeffrey Dahmer confessed that their rampages started with viewing porn at an early age.

Companies have done productivity studies to determine how much it costs their business while employees are searching porn sites rather than producing at their jobs. According to Porn Harm Research, 20 percent of men and 13 percent of women admit to watching porn online while at work. The generally accepted cost figure in time lost, in America alone, seems to be in the annual range of $16 billion to $17 billion.

Some Staggering Statistics

- Every second 28,258 users are watching pornography on the Internet.

- Every second $3,075 is being spent on pornography on the Internet.

- Every second 372 people are typing the word "adult" into search engines.

- 40 million Americans regularly visit porn sites.

- One-third of porn viewers are women.

- Search engines get 116,000 queries every day related to child Pornography. (This statistic is taken from "The Effects of Pornography on Individuals, Marriage, Family, and Community," by Patrick F. Fagan, Ph.D., psychologist, and former Deputy Assistant Health and Human Services Secretary.)

The U.S. Department of Justice provides more details from its Office of Justice Programs fact sheet:

- In recent studies, 49,105 human trafficking victims worldwide were identified, a 59 percent increase over the previous reporting year.

- At the time of this report, an estimated 12.3 million adults and children were in forced labor, bonded labor, and forced prostitution around the world; 56 percent of these victims were women and girls. (Almost a decade after statistics in this category were reported, we now see an exponential increase in these numbers.)

The internet has become the Pandora's box for the porn industry. The Porn Harm Research, directed by the National Center on Sexual Exploitation, gives us a stunning and hard-to-believe look into the numbers.

- 12 percent of all websites are pornographic

- 2.5 billion e-mails each day are pornographic in nature (8 percent of daily traffic)

- 25 percent of search engine requests are pornographic-related

- only 3 percent of adult websites require age verification

- 150,000 new escort ads are posted online every day

- the least favorite day of the year for viewing porn is Thanksgiving

- *the most popular day of the week for viewing porn is Sunday*

The tremendous demand for more of this horrible sin helps to fuel the human-trafficking industry. From child pornography on up, the purveyors of this wickedness seek out whom they can capture and sell into the marketplace of these insatiable desires. More than 75 percent of underage victims—children—are advertised online.

The Alliance For Freedom, Restoration, and Justice (AFRJ)

AFRJ is at the forefront of fighting human trafficking worldwide. Their Engage Together initiative (www.engagetogether.com) has been created to end human trafficking and help the vulnerable. (I encourage you to visit their site to understand this horrible and pervasive evil.) According to AFRJ, worldwide more than 40 million souls are modern-day slaves and are being sold for labor, sexual exploitation, and organs. Human trafficking is an evil that is happening not just around the world, but also in nearly every community throughout the United States, *with as many as 300,000 children in the U.S. at risk of commercial sexual exploitation each year.* The 300,000 number translates to an average of 6,000 children *per state* used for nefarious purposes *each year*. They are used not only for the sexual pleasures of perverts, but around the world they are kidnapped for the harvesting of their organs and become the modern-day slaves of child labor.

Pornography fuels the lurid imaginations of wicked men. Hundreds of thousands of Americans and millions of others worldwide have become addicted to this disastrous demon. It is of great interest to find that the first time the word "wickedness" is found in the Bible, it is located in the story of Noah and the flood (Genesis 6:5): "And God saw that the *wickedness* of man was great in the earth and that every imagination of the thoughts of his heart was only evil continually." The Scriptures say God was grieved in His heart over this outcome and He destroyed the earth by water. The lost world tries to deny this flood ever happened. They set their opinions over the stated truth of Scripture so they can justify their thoughts and imaginations. Peter, in at least two clear verses, told us it would happen. 1 Peter 3:20: "Which sometime were disobedient when once the longsuffering of God waited in the days of Noah, while the ark was a preparing, wherein few, that is, eight souls were saved by water." 2 Peter 3:5: "For this *they willingly are ignorant* of, that by the word of God the heavens were of old, and the earth standing out of the water and in the water: Whereby the world that then was, being overflowed with water, perished."

The world today continues to readily accept and propagate the flood as a myth. This helps to sooth consciences into believing there will be no judgment to come. Don't miss the glaring truth. Judgment came when wickedness abounded. God destroyed the world once. Will He do it again? Peter continued his warning in answer to this very question. 2 Peter 3:7: "But the heavens and the earth, which are now, by the same word are kept in store, *reserved unto fire against the day of judgment* and perdition of ungodly men." Men's ungodliness led to the first time that the Lord judged the whole earth. It will be men's wickedness that will lead to the last time God will destroy the earth. It is not a matter of *if* it will happen, only a matter of *when*. It is the belief of this writer that the downward spiral of the morality of man is fast approaching the Days of Noah. Jesus said (Luke 17:26): "And *as it was in the days of Noah,* so shall it be also in the days of the Son of man." His judgment is coming, and it is coming sooner rather than later.

2. **Prostitution**: Leviticus 19:29: "Do not *prostitute* thy daughter, to cause her *to be a whore; lest the land fall to whoredom and the land become full of wickedness.*"

Some of the international cultures of today are still engaged in this awful sin in which a parent sells his or her daughter to another. This despicable act tramples the most sacred of relations, that which should naturally exist between a parent and his or her child. The practice is nothing less than complete and utter wickedness. Thus prostitution in its broader definition runs rampant worldwide.

Consider the reports that came out of Rio de Janeiro during the World Cup and the Olympics. Prostitution in Brazil is legal. The DailyMail.com released an article on July 4, 2016, depicting the lower-than-expected turnout for prostitution during the World Cup. Because of the slump in demand, the prostitutes were offering a "supermarket sale" complete with "menus" of discounted rates.

News.com.au reported on July 24, 2016: "On a bend on one of Brazil's longest highways, only a 50-minute drive from Rio de Janeiro's Olympic village, *girls as young as nine* are selling their bodies to truck drivers for money [emphases in this section are mine — M.S.].

Just a few kilometers from the glittering new stadiums where the world's elite athletes are gathering to battle it out for Olympic gold is a miserable world of poverty, violence, and child exploitation.

The BR-116 runs for 4600 km between the World Cup stadium host city Fortaleza in the far north of Brazil to Brazil's largest city, Sao Paulo, where the Arena de Corinthians staged Olympic soccer games in the south.

The road is nicknamed the Highway of Death (Rodovia da Morte) for its mortality rate due to many accidents and unstable weather and conditions along the route. But its real misery occurs at 262 truck stops along its way, *where female children are sold for sex, often by their own families,* sometimes as part of a town's unofficial bartering system."

HUMAN TRAFFICKING

The buying and selling of men, women, boys, and girls has become the scourge of the twenty-first century. The worldwide sales figures in human trafficking exceeds $150 billion a year. The Forbes 500 report for 2018 helps place trafficking numbers in perspective. A billion and a half dollars is more in one year than the combined annual revenues for Disney, FedEx, and Coca Cola.

Buyers drive the market that makes child sexual exploitation a moneymaker for traffickers. Never have the words of the Bible rung more authentic than when it says (1 Timothy 6:10): "For the love of money is the root of all evil: which while some coveted after, they have erred from the faith, and pierced themselves through with many sorrows." Rarely do buyers face serious consequences. Instead, children are being charged with prostitution, but there is no such thing as a child prostitute. Children cannot consent to sex. They are *victims, not criminals.* Statistics provided by THORN(a website dedicated to defending children from sexual abuse) state that approximately one thousand American children are arrested for prostitution every year.

As the trafficked child goes in and out of the legal system, they reach the age of an adult (provided they live that long). Then, when those victims are arrested, their criminal record prevents them from accessing critical resources like housing or jobs. This prevents them from creating the stability they need to avoid further exploitation. New York was the first state to pass a law allowing trafficking survivors to clear their record for prostitution offenses, and Florida later passed a bill enabling survivors to expunge their record for any crime committed during their trafficking situation.

America has legalized the selling of women in some corners of the country. Many choose to be in the business of selling themselves willingly. Others are unwilling participants in this cesspool of sin. Prostitution is not a glamorous life that ends well as depicted by Hollywood in such movies as *Pretty Woman*.

Forced prostitution is the backbone of human trafficking. This evil is the new form of slavery across our borders. Our land has fallen to whoredom and is full of wickedness. Women and children are kidnapped and thrown into this mill of catastrophe. Taken against their will, they are outcasts to those who use them, and to the society from which they were snatched. They have no one to turn to—and according to most statistics, they have only seven to nine years before they will die from its horrors.

The circle goes round and round. They are kidnapped. They are drugged. They are sold (in many cases, ten to twenty times a night). They get arrested and charged with a felony that stays on their record. Their pimp (or kidnapper) bails them out, and they are thrown right back into the swamp of exploitation. New laws are being discussed and written by state Attorney Generals across our continent to deal with this complex issue. Not all prostitutes are willing participants. The legal system is trying to play catch-up to make the distinction.

Lives are ruined, families are destroyed, and souls are discarded like trash. It is no wonder the Lord sees prostitution as wickedness.

3. **Perversions:** Leviticus 18:22: "Thou shalt not lie with mankind, as with womankind: it is abomination." Leviticus 18:23: "Neither shalt thou lie with any beast to defile thyself therewith: neither shall any woman stand before a beast to lie down thereto: it is confusion."

When God says that something is an abomination, it is not to be taken lightly.

Webster's New World College Dictionary, Third Edition, defines abomination as "something greatly hated and loathed." The mental image produced from the description in the above verses is disgusting, Let's approach the second verse first.

a.   **Bestiality:** In almost all circles of conversation today, the idea of having sexual activities with an animal is still considered atrocious. That being said, it does not mean that this perversion is nonexistent.

In August 2009, an article appeared, written by Thomas Francis, reporting on a specific issue of bestiality. In his narrative, entitled "Those Who Practice Bestiality Say They're Part of the Next Sexual Rights Movement," Francis relays a story of an admitted "zoophile."

"During his sophomore year in high school, (name withheld by this author) finally got fed up with hearing homophobic cracks. If his classmates thought being gay was weird (he was openly bisexual), he had a confession that would blow their minds. He told them he is sexually attracted to dogs and horses. 'I just couldn't keep it in anymore,' he says. 'Just for the hell of it, I figured I'd throw it out there and have them make fun of me even more.' Which they did. An 18-year-old from Arizona who graduated from high school this past year, he says classmates taunted him by calling him Bestiality Dude.

Being a 'zoophile' in modern American society, he says, is 'like being gay in the 1950s. You feel like you have to hide, that if you say it out loud, people will look at you like a freak.'"

Of course, the Internet can be used for shocking evils and is slowly making headway to normalize this abomination. It has allowed those involved in bestiality around the world to interact—not only to exchange their sensual cravings but also to form alliances and develop strategies for the political battle.

Bestiality is a cringe-worthy topic that no one wants to discuss, including this author. But, as this group of so-called "zoophiles" gains confidence, the push for society to become more "tolerant" of their "lifestyle" choice will follow. It is only a matter of time before they become more open and outspoken in their demands to live their life the way they see fit without discrimination. (Haven't we heard that argument before . . . anywhere else?) Unbelievable as it may sound now, bestiality may become the next civil rights movement. Isaiah 5:20: "Woe unto them *that call evil good, and good evil*; that put darkness for light, and light for darkness; that put bitter for sweet, and sweet for bitter!"

As cave drawings confirm, there has always been a carnal desire in mankind's vilest yearnings to lie with beasts. The Bible says (Ecclesiastes 1:9): "The thing that hath been, it is that which shall be; and that which is done is that which shall be done: and *there is no new thing under the sun.*"

Another report from the Daily Mail tells this grotesque story. Headline:

"Beastiality Brothels Are Spreading Through Germany Faster Than Ever Thanks to a Law That Makes Animal Porn Illegal But Sex with Animals Legal, a Livestock Protection Officer Has Warned."

Madeleine Martin told the Frankfurter *Rundschau* that current laws are not protecting animals from predatory zoophiles who are increasingly able to turn to bestiality as a "lifestyle choice." A "lifestyle choice" sounds familiar, does it not?

She highlighted one case in which a farmer in the Gross-Gerau region of southwest Germany noticed his once friendly flock of sheep was beginning to shy away from human contact. So he rigged a CCTV camera in the rafters of his barn to discover multiple men sneaking in during the night to abuse his beloved livestock sexually.

The wretchedness of the human heart knows no end. Before any of us think too highly of ourselves, let us remember that given the right set of circumstances and enough time, we would all be capable of any sin. That is what the Lord means when He says we are desperately wicked.

We don't have to go back as far as 2009 or as far away as Germany to find this evil conduct. According to Fox News, on June 4, 2018, a Michigan State University health physicist was charged with two counts of sodomy for allegedly committing bestiality with a basset hound. (*The Lansing State Journal* reported this incident.)

Sexual contact between humans and animals is a disgusting and horrific concept. It makes one wonder if there is anything our society will reject as being just plain wrong! God's Word has not changed, but oh how our civilization believes it has evolved. Bestiality is a subject not talked about in polite society, nor *does it need to be*. In most conversations today, the topic of humans lying with animals still makes people recoil. This wickedness, however, is reaching its tentacles to a world headed toward depravity. The book of Job asks a piercing question: "Is not thy *wickedness* great? And thine iniquities infinite?" (Job 22:5). This verse is worth contemplating. The sins of man are not just wicked, they are *great wickedness*. The word *infinite* is used in this verse in God's Word to show us that our sinful nature knows no bounds. When it comes to bestiality, that seems to be most evident.

> b. **Homosexuality:** As much as we might recoil from a discussion on bestiality, we barely squirm when the conversation switches to homosexuality. These two sins are placed adjacent to each other in Scripture! If the one sin should be shunned, then so should the other. Leviticus 20:13: "If a man also lie with mankind, as he lieth with a woman, both of them have committed an abomination."

What is the final authority on the matter? When it comes down to it, what is it that the homosexual, and those who champion their lifestyle, use to comfort themselves in their beliefs? Where does their view originate? On what do they base their judgments?

FINAL AUTHORITY

The lost world does not believe that the final authority on moral matters is the Bible. Their final authority is themselves. The homosexual's confidence in what they believe comes from other sources. Their final authority is:

1. **Their opinion:** they believe what they believe. They are their own authority. It is difficult to have a discussion with them because there is no basis for what they think. It is just what they believe, and they will argue that they have as much right to their opinion as anyone else. The resolution of an argument of opinions will generally degrade to a battle of wills, and he who has the stronger resolve tends to walk away as the self-anointed winner.

   Anyone who believes they have won the argument on behalf of the homosexual lifestyle is tragically mistaken. They have convinced the sinner that there is nothing to worry about. Homosexuals are told there is nothing wrong with exercising their right to live as they see fit. They are told they will not face any judgment in hell for what they do. It must be stated that, to pat someone on the back while on their way to damnation is *not* a show of love. The audacity of the defenders of the LGBTQ way of life to say they "care" about those involved in what God calls *abomination!* Human opinion is never to take precedence over the divine revelation of God.

2. **Their emotions:** they base their decisions on morality on how they "feel" about the issue. They measure the opposing Christian viewpoint by the same standard. The homosexual thinks that if someone has an opposing view, then that person must automatically be angry or hateful or fearful. Thus the word "homophobic" is introduced. They applaud themselves as having the more "honorable" emotions of "tolerance" and "caring" and "love" for the other person.

   It should be stated here that Christians do not hate homosexuals. We are not angry at them nor are we afraid of them. We are disgusted with the demonic attempts to legitimize what the Bible explicitly calls sin. *It is the true Christian who cares about the homosexual.* We see them as souls made in God's image like everyone else. We believe they are in grave danger if they will not repent. We comprehend the awfulness of their sin, and we know the *terror of the Lord*, and just as assuredly we recognize His willingness to save any who might repent. Waving the flag of warning is the real display of concern for those in danger. The Scriptures warn us all of things that can destroy us and send us to an eternal punishment. Jude 1:7: "Even as Sodom and Gomorrah, and the cities about them in like manner, giving themselves over to fornication, and *going after strange flesh*, are set forth for an example, *suffering the vengeance of eternal fire*." It should not go unnoticed that the first time the word *wicked* appears in Scripture is found in Genesis 13:13: "But the men of Sodom were *wicked* and sinners before the Lord exceedingly."

The sexual acts of men with men and women with women are a violation of purity. The carnal actions of the gay and lesbian offenders are a gross infringement on the very nature of God. Romans 1 is clear about this (verses 26, 27): "For this cause God gave them up unto vile affections: for even their women did change the natural use into that which is *against nature*: And likewise also the men, leaving the natural use of the woman, burned in their lust one toward another; men with men working that which is unseemly, and receiving in themselves that recompence of their error which was meet."

If LGBTQ individuals insist on defending their lifestyle choices, there is nothing left for the Lord to do but turn them over to themselves to be destroyed. Read carefully, continuing in Romans 1:28-32: "And even as they did not like to retain God in their knowledge, *God gave them over to a reprobate mind*, to do those things which are not convenient; Being filled with all unrighteousness, fornication, *wickedness*, covetousness, maliciousness; full of envy, murder, debate, deceit, malignity; whisperers, Backbiters, haters of God, despiteful, proud, boasters, inventors of evil things, disobedient to parents, Without understanding, covenant-breakers, *without natural affection,* implacable, unmerciful: *Who knowing the judgment of God,* that they which commit such things are worthy of death, not only do the same but have pleasure in them that do them." They did not want to think about or recall what the Lord has said on the matter of sin. The dictionary defines *reprobate* as someone who is a depraved, unprincipled, or wicked person: a person rejected by God and beyond hope of salvation. Pay close attention to this: it is God who uses the word *reprobate.*

This passage covers more sins than just sodomy and fornication. The Bible proclaims that all of us are sinners. There is not anyone righteous. Romans 3:10: "As it is written, *There is none righteous,* no, not one." When it comes to sin, we are not graded on a curve in which those who sin less make it into Heaven and those who sin more go to hell. All have come short of the glory of God and the Lord groups us together when it comes to sin. James 2:10: "For whosoever shall keep the whole law, and yet offend in one point, *he is guilty of all.*"

No one knows better than a Christian (who has been born again by the Spirit of God) how lost we were before we were saved, and how blessed we are to be forgiven for our sins. It is with that gratefulness in our hearts that we try to share with the gay community the incredible offer of salvation. That salvation can come only if there is the admission of guilt and a heartfelt prayer for forgiveness.

3. **Their inclinations:** the argument we hear so often is, "I was born that way."

Let's look at the logic behind that statement. God says that for men to lie with men and women to lie with women is sin. He is clear that anyone involved in this activity is worthy of death and eternal damnation. If the homosexual is "born that way," but God calls it sin, then that would make God an unjust God. The Lord would not create man to be the very thing that He calls an abomination. That would make God an evil god who no one would desire to worship. Job 34:10: "Therefore hearken unto me, ye men of under-standing: *far be it from God, that he should do wickedness*; and from the Almighty, that he should commit iniquity."

We are all born with inclinations to sin. Whatever our tendencies may be, these are our sin weaknesses. Different people are tempted by different things. One person is tempted to steal while another is tempted to drunkenness. As stated earlier, if we sin at all then we are guilty of all. It does not matter which is our particular weakness. If we give in to that temptation it is sin. We are not sinners because we sin, we sin because we are already sinners. We have been born under that curse.

The heterosexual is born with sinful tendencies. When it comes to fleshly desires, he or she is tempted to fulfill his or her lusts outside of the institution of marriage. God has ordained marriage and prohibited sexual relations outside of that institution. The heterosexual is warned within the Ten Commandments not to commit adultery. Just because an individual has impulses toward the same sex does not negate what the Bible says.

That brings us to face the truth about what we use as our *final authority*. Is it our opinion or our emotions or our compulsions—or is it the Word of God? The Word of God has the ability to search the depths of man's heart. 1 Corinthians 2:10: "For the Spirit searcheth all things, yea, the deep things of God." The Bible opens spiritual eyes that men might see the truth. We should want the Lord to reveal to us His insight on the law. He is asking us to live according to its principles. Psalms 119:18: "*Open thou mine eyes, that I may behold wondrous things out of thy law.*" If we let the Word of God search our hearts and open our eyes, then the Scriptures have the power to bring us together with our Creator in all areas of our lives. Our thoughts should be His thoughts. Our desires should be His desires. God is the one who is perfect. We are to be perfect as He is perfect. Isaiah 1:18, 19: "Come now, and let us reason together, saith the Lord: though your sins be as scarlet, they shall be as white as snow; though they be red like crimson, they shall be as wool, If ye be willing and obedient.

Here is what the Bible teaches on the matter of homosexuality.

a. **It is an abomination:** Do not ignore that word. That is the precise way God determined to convey His mind-set on the matter. The God who created us all declares it is both disgusting and detestable, revolting and abhorrent.

b. **It is described:** Leviticus 18:22: "Thou shalt not lie with mankind, as with womankind: it is abomination." The New Testament book of Romans continues the thought (Romans 1:26, 27): "For this cause God gave them up unto vile affections: for even *their women did change the natural use into that which is against nature:* And likewise *also the men, leaving the natural use of the woman, burned in their lust one toward another; men with men working that which is unseemly,* and receiving in themselves that recompence of their error which was meet." God established the standard. Violation of God's commands will lead to judgment. Romans 1:32: "Who knowing *the judgment of God,* that they which commit such things are worthy of death, not only do the same, but have pleasure in them that do them."

c. **It appears in a list of sins next to bestiality** (Leviticus 18:22, 23): "Thou shalt not lie with mankind, as with womankind: it is abomination. Neither shalt thou lie with any beast to defile thyself therewith: neither shall any woman stand before a beast to lie down thereto: it is confusion." Sin is sin whether we find it disgusting or not. The fact that parades are held and laws are changed to benefit those choosing the sin of homosexuality alters nothing when it comes to God's declarations on the matter.

d. **It has been punished harshly, by God, in the past** (Jude 7): "Even as Sodom and Gomorrah, and the cities about them in like manner, giving themselves over to fornication, and going after strange flesh, are *set forth for an example*, suffering the vengeance of eternal fire. The destruction of these two cities was an example to all the generations to follow, including ours.

e. **It will be punished more dramatically in the future.** Jesus put it this way (Mark 6:11): "And whosoever shall not receive you, nor hear you, when ye depart thence, shake off the dust under your feet. *It shall be more tolerable for Sodom and Gomorrah in the day of judgment, than for that city*."

f. **It is condemned in both the Old and New testaments.** The argument cannot be made that the topic is found only in the Old Testament. Here are some passages to consider: Leviticus 18:22; Leviticus 20:13; Genesis 19:5; Judges 19:22; 1 Kings 14:24; Romans 1:26, 27; 1 Corinthians 6:9; 1 Timothy 1:10; Jude 7.

g. *It is not the unforgivable sin.* 1 John 1:9: "If we confess our sins, he is faithful and just to forgive us our sins, and to cleanse us from all unrighteousness." Those involved in this sin can be saved. But time will run out on them if they persist in their wicked ways. Sin ripens the sinner for destruction. This is why the Lord said He would turn them over to a reprobate mind. He recognizes that there comes a point in the degeneration of the soul that there is no hope of it returning to Him. Knowing the *terror of the Lord* that was played out on Sodom and Gomorrah, it would seem that a quick response to the Lord's offer of mercy would be fitting. All sinners should recognize the lateness of the hour and pray earnestly that the Lord will acknowledge their pleas for mercy, grace, and forgiveness. 2 Corinthians 6:2: "For he saith, I have heard thee *in a time accepted*, and in the day of salvation have I succoured thee: behold, now is the accepted time; behold, now is the day of salvation."

Every person born has a decision to make. We can choose to sin or we can choose to repent of our sin. The Bible is the final authority on what is and what is not sin. All sins can be forgiven. All sins are to be judged.

The believer's sin was judged on the cross more than two thousand years ago. The unbelievers will face judgment in the near future. Today is the day to decide which choice to make because we may not have tomorrow. Today can be the day of salvation. God's way is a choice.

We either choose to follow Him or we decide to follow our way. But time is quickly running out.

> "Let the **heathen** be wakened, and come up to the valley
> of Jehoshaphat: for **there will I sit to judge all the
> heathen** round about. Put ye in the sickle, for the harvest
> is ripe: come, get you down; for the press is full, the fats
> overflow; for their **wickedness** is great. **Multitudes,
> multitudes in the valley of decision: for the day of the
> Lord is near in the valley of decision** (Joel 3:12-14.)

CHAPTER ELEVEN
— A CUP OF GOD'S WRATH —

*"The same shall drink of the wine of the **wrath of God**, which is poured out without mixture into **the cup** of his indignation; and he shall be tormented with fire and brimstone in the presence of the holy angels and in the presence of the Lamb (Revelation 14:10).*

The premise of this book is that there is not much "fire and brimstone" preaching anymore. Good men of God who are willing to tackle the subject are met with resistance. Ministers are hearing from the churchgoers that the congregations are "too educated for such antiquated messages." Their argument gets extended to statements like, "Those hell, fire, and brimstone sermons are not a way to build a church." It is not the preacher's job to put people in the pews. It is the preacher's job to put power in the pulpit! He is not to appease the lost but to preach the Word. God is in charge of adding to His church as sinners get saved. Preaching is man's mandate from God. Salvation is the Lord's miracle to men.

Many people do not believe in hell because they think it is a disproportionate response from a loving God to His fallen creation.

But saying there is no eternal punishment in a fire that burns forever makes three faulty assumptions.

1. That the Word of God, the Bible, is not valid or not to be taken literally.
2. That God is not a holy and just God who will punish sin.
3. That man is not as depraved as the Scriptures seem to describe.

It is no surprise that the unbelievers do not want to hear about eternal damnation. If there is one ounce of conviction left in the lost hearts of man, the preaching of punishment ought to stir the fear of the Lord within them. It will take some hard preaching to shake them from their slumber. This generation has been saturated with sermons on the love of God. As a result, messages on fire and brimstone are foreign to them. There is nothing wrong with preaching God's love, but there are a lot of lost souls that have not responded to that message. It is time to balance our description of Almighty God with His justice and judgment. The hope is that some who have not responded to the "love message" will react with repentance to the "judgment message." Psalms 11:6: "Upon *the wicked*, he shall rain snares, *fire, and brimstone,* and an horrible tempest: this shall be the portion of their *cup.*"

Unbelievers today are sitting on a fence. On one side of the fence are the green pastures of God's mercy and grace. On the other side of the fence are the dried branches of thorns and briers prepared for the Lord's judgment and wrath. Jesus said (John 15:6): "If a man abide not in me, he is cast forth as a branch, and is withered; and men gather them and *cast them into the fire, and they are burned.*" Isaiah put it this way (Isaiah 10:17): "And the light of Israel shall be for a fire, and his Holy One for a flame: and it shall burn and devour his *thorns and his briers* in one day." The still waters of God's love are waiting. So also are the raging seas of His fury. There comes a time when we must get off the fence.

The storm clouds of judgment are gathering. The true church of the Lord Jesus Christ longs to see its *King*. Christians have been praying for more than two thousand years for God's kingdom to come and His will to be done here on earth as it is in Heaven. The gospel has been preached in the world. Printing presses have produced Bibles and tracts in hundreds of languages. Satellites have beamed the message of salvation all over the earth. The time is drawing near for the fire to be lit. Christians are looking for the Rapture of the church. We do not want any to perish, but we are ready to go home. The prayer is going up: "*How long, Lord?* Wilt thou hide thyself <u>for ever</u>? Shall *thy wrath burn like fire?* (Psalms 89:46) The answer to the prayer is: a little while. Hebrews 10:37: "For yet *a little while* and he that shall come will come, and will not tarry." *Even so, Lord Jesus, come quickly!*

THE INHABITANTS OF THE EARTH

Each time the phrase "the inhabitants of the earth" is used, it refers to lost people. After the church has been removed all the remaining people will fall into the category of "the inhabitants of the earth." The Bible calls this the time of Jacob's trouble. It is described it as the Day of the Lord. It will be the time of tribulation and great tribulation. Those on this earth will stand in awe as they see the sword of judgment coming upon this planet and upon them. The punishment they did not believe in will begin. Jeremiah 25:29: "Ye shall not be unpunished: for I will call for a sword upon all *the inhabitants of the earth*, saith the Lord of hosts."

How many warnings has the Lord given to lost man? The Bible is His Word, and it is filled with cautions from the Lord indicating judgment ahead. Many other books have been written like this one, books informing the lost and serving notice that Jesus will be coming back soon and that He will be pouring out the wrath of God. Jesus will have a sharp sickle in His hand because it will be harvesttime. None of the inhabitants of the earth will be able to ask: "What is He doing?" They will know what is about to happen. Daniel 4:35: "And *all the inhabitants of the earth* are reputed as nothing: and he doeth according to his will in the army of heaven, and among the inhabitants of the earth: and none can stay his hand, or say unto him, What doest thou?" They will hide themselves in the rocks and caves of the earth knowing it is the Son of God and that He is coming to take vengeance upon them. Revelation 6:14-17: "And the heaven departed as a scroll when it is rolled together, and every mountain and island were moved out of their places. And the kings of the earth, and the great men, and the rich men, and the chief captains, and the mighty men, and every bondman, and every free man [in other words, "the inhabitants of the earth" – M.S.] hid themselves in the dens and in the rocks of the mountains; And said to the mountains and rocks, Fall on us, and hide us from the face of him that sitteth on the throne, and from the wrath of the Lamb: *For the great day of his wrath is come; and who shall be able to stand?*" Every nation will suffer the awful judgement of God. Jeremiah 25:15: "For thus saith the Lord God of Israel unto me; Take the wine cup of this fury at my hand, and cause *all the nations*, to whom I send thee, to drink it."

The devastation described in many passages of Scripture is unimaginable. All the destruction will come from just *one cup* of His wrath. If the Lord were to use all of His fury, the universe would be dissolved. As mankind hides himself from what is to come, he is asking the question: "Who shall be able to stand?" It is a rhetorical question. No one can stand against the *Lord Jesus Christ!*

ABORTION

This world has continuously worked to change the laws of God to suit its fancies. The commandment says: "Thou shalt not kill." The proverbs say that God hates the shedding of innocent blood. How could a civilized society come to the place of legalized abortion? The answer, of course, is a total ignoring of what the Bible says is correct and an exaltation of what humanity desires to be true. We have heard the argument of the abortion advocates. Some of their rationale is wrapped up in the "what if?" category.

1. What if the woman is a victim of rape?
2. What if the woman is a victim of incest?
3. What if the woman's life is in danger due to pregnancy?
4. What if the fetus has a severe abnormality?

Take a close look at what one state discovered. Florida records a reason for every abortion that occurs within its borders each year. In 2015, there were 71,740 abortions in Florida. This table lists each cause and the percentage of abortions that happened because of it.

Percentage	Reason
.001%	The pregnancy resulted from an incestuous relationship.
.065%	The woman's life was endangered by the pregnancy.
.085%	The woman was raped.
.288%	The woman's physical health was threatened by the pregnancy.
.294%	The woman's psychological health was threatened by the pregnancy.
.666%	There was a serious fetal abnormality.
6.268%	The woman aborted for social or economic reasons.
92.33%	No reason (elective) was stated.

— Statistics are from the Guttmacher Institute

Let's extrapolate the numbers. If we add the percentages of the first six categories mentioned above, we find that 1.399% of abortions performed in Florida fell into that "what if" list. That means that 98.6% of the abortions were for less than "legitimate" reasons. Even if we accept the premise that the six top categories are good reasons to end the pregnancy, it means that only 1,004 babies needed to be aborted. Of the 71,740 babies that did die, 70,736 toddlers could have been celebrating their third birthdays this year. These numbers will vary some from state to state, but the trend is substantiated and undeniable.

But the inhabitants of the earth have changed God's Law. They made abortion legal. And for that, they will be burned. These words are harsh, but they are the words of Isaiah the prophet. Isaiah 24:5: "The earth also is defiled under the inhabitants thereof; because they have transgressed the laws, *changed the ordinance*, broken the everlasting covenant. Therefore hath the curse devoured the earth, and they that dwell therein are desolate: therefore *the inhabitants of the earth are burned*, and few men left."

Abortion is not the unforgivable sin. Those who have had an abortion can be saved. Those who have performed abortions still have time to respond to the invitation of grace. Those who have helped to get laws passed to legalize this savage practice can return to the Lord who made them and still be reconciled to him. That is the magnificent mercy of God. All they need to do is admit that God is right and they are wrong and ask His forgiveness and repent. However, if they continue with their assertion that they are right and God is false, there remains no hope for them. There is only the ever-present danger of falling into the hands of the living God. What a dreadful end. Hebrews 10:31: "It is a fearful thing to fall into the hands of the living God."

Another travesty of debate is the constant questioning of the "viability" of the unborn child during different trimesters. All of this discussion is an attempt by the anti-life crowd to allow abortions to be conducted later and later in pregnancy. The question boils down to: "When does life begin?" The Bible says that life is in the blood. Leviticus 17:11: "For the life of the flesh is in the blood." Science believes that the heart of an embryo begins to beat at twenty-three days. *If we declare a person dead when the heart stops beating, shouldn't we declare a person alive when the heart starts beating?*

Most pro-life advocates believe life begins at conception. This is probably the case as God sees it, but even if it is twenty-three days later, that is long before any of us knows that another tiny life even exists. That little human being is well on its way before we recognize its presence in this world. God hates the shedding of innocent blood.

Once again, the Bible proves to be true. The inhabitants of the earth have brought this curse to the whole world. It is estimated that 25 million babies are aborted worldwide each year. The fire of God's wrath is lit, and His fury has been ignited. The angels are stirring the fuels of hell in preparation for the disposal of a lost humanity. Deuteronomy 32:22: "For a fire is kindled in mine anger, *and shall burn unto the lowest hell*, and shall consume the earth with her increase, and *set on fire the foundations of the mountains.* The volcanoes of this world are about to blow their tops. From the peaks along the ring of fire to the unseen cauldron of Yellowstone, this world is about to explode. The time to cry for mercy is quickly running out.

Christians need to be warning the lost. The lost need to start listening. The Scriptures are saying that the time is fast approaching when God is going to wrap things up as it concerns the sin and rebellion of man. It is time to evaluate where we stand and if we stand with the Lord. (1 Corinthians 11:28: "But let a man *examine himself.*") Backslidden Christians need to weigh the price of apostasy. The unsaved should consider their foolish ways before it is too late. The warnings of the Bible are absolute. The Lord waits because his mercy is longsuffering. But He is not obligated to delay. Many have heard the forewarnings before. They wrongfully assume that if nothing has happened so far, then there is nothing to be alarmed about. They are "at peace with the world"—and that is precisely the problem.

It is time for all people to return to the churches to hear the truth. It is time that the pulpits are again pounded with fists of fire. Deuteronomy 31:12: "Gather the people together, men, and women, and children, and thy stranger that is within thy gates, that they may hear, and that they may learn, *and fear the Lord your God,* and observe to do all the words of this law." The cup of His fury will soon be poured out. Call upon the Lord before He tips that cup. Consider your soul. There is still time to choose which cup you will drink. Will it be the cup of trembling or the cup of salvation? The psalmist made the right choice; will you? Psalms 116:13: "I will take *the cup of salvation, and call upon the name of the Lord.*"

The Lord is in preparation for the gathering of those who are trusting in Him. Psalms 50:4-6: "He shall call to the heavens from above, and to the earth, that he may judge his people. *Gather my saints together unto me*; those that have made a covenant with me by sacrifice. And the heavens shall declare his righteousness: for God is judge himself." There will be the gathering of the saints, and there will be a gathering of the sinners. God knows who are His and who are not. He will divide them for their reward, whether it be for good or whether it be for evil. 2 Peter 2:9: "The Lord knoweth how to deliver the godly out of temptations, and to reserve the unjust unto the day of judgment to be punished."

Jesus is coming to sweep up the dust of man's disobedience. It will be house-cleaning Heaven-style. All rebellion will be removed to the fiery furnaces of hell. Matthew 3:12: "Whose fan is in his hand, and he will *thoroughly purge his floor*, and gather his wheat into the garner; *but he will burn up the chaff with unquenchable fire.*" For those who say God is not like this depiction, take a close look at the beginning of this last verse. He will not only send defiant men to hell, He will *fan the flames.*

For the last century, preaching topics have centered on the love of God. The emphasis on God's mercy and grace rather than His holiness and judgment may be in direct response to the hell, fire, and brimstone preaching of another generation. But the pendulum that swings from His kindness to His anger has hovered over the former without swaying back to the latter for too long. The message of love has been preached to the extreme at the neglect of God's attributes of hatred toward sin and His disapproval of those intent on transgressing His laws.

We are *not* talking about two different gods here. We are speaking of the one true God and His revealed character. The appeal of His loving nature would be less attractive if He allowed the misery of sin to continue forever. The holy and just quality of His righteousness demands an end to unrighteousness. God the Father showed His wrath and anger against sin when Jesus, who knew no sin, became our sin that we could then become the righteousness of God in Him. He has waited patiently, generation after generation, for this truth to sink in. But the end of this dispensation of grace is very near.

When the Lord decides that the clock has struck midnight on His longsuffering, He will implement tremendous retribution on remaining mankind. Ezekiel 25:17: "And *I will execute great vengeance upon them with furious rebukes*; and they shall know that I am the Lord *when I shall lay my vengeance upon them*." It is a mockery to the character of God that this truth has been ignored.

The Lamb's book of life will be closed one day. There will be no more time to add another name to the registry of the saved. It is the conjecture of this author that the Lamb's book will have many blank pages left within its covers. The empty spaces will have left plenty of room for the addition of any name that might have called upon the Lord before it was too late.

Not only will the book be shut, but God's offer of forgiveness will have concluded, Heaven's doors will have been secured, the courts of God's mercy will have been stamped inaccessible, and the ears of God will be closed. Micah 3:4: "Then shall they cry unto the Lord, *but he will not hear them: he will even hide his face from them at that time*, as they have behaved themselves ill in their doings." Those who hid their face from Him will now have Him conceal his face from them.

There is still time to be saved. There is still time to procure salvation for your soul. But there is precious little of that time left. Is there anyone left who will come to the Lord? Jesus himself wondered (Luke 18:8): "Nevertheless when the Son of man cometh, shall he find faith on the earth?"

When Jesus comes back to punish the people of the world for their sins, it will be a bloody affair. It is difficult to picture our Lord in a blood-filled avenging role. Again, we must turn to Scripture rather than to any preconceived representation of God that we might hold. Isaiah 26:21: "For, behold, the Lord cometh out of his place to punish the inhabitants of the earth for their iniquity: *the earth also shall disclose her blood*, and shall no more cover her slain." Again, the Bible tells us, in Revelation 19:13: "And he [Jesus] was clothed with a vesture *dipped in blood*: and his name is called The Word of God." This may sound grotesque to some. Even this author wishes that it were not so. But ask yourself this question: "Why wouldn't Jesus, who shed His blood for those who would accept Him, not shed the blood of those who would reject Him? There will be no cup of wrath without blood. The crucifixion was a bloody day, and so shall the day of vengeance be as well. Psalms 58:10: "The righteous shall rejoice when he seeth the *vengeance*: he shall wash his feet *in the blood of the wicked*."

Oh, the innocent blood that has been spilled on this earth. From the blameless blood of Abel to the guiltless blood of the Son of God, history has soaked the soil with the virtue of God's anointed. From the spotless blood of the disciples to the pure blood of those martyred for their faith in the Lord, the earth has groaned for justice. Romans 8:22: "For we know that the whole *creation groaneth* and travaileth in pain together until now." The earthquakes that shake this world and the volcanoes that erupt without warning are dramatic evidence of this visible yearning from His creation. Storms, tornadoes, floods, and tsunamis are the cry of the earth for God to come and restore to this planet the perfection of the Garden of Eden.

At the end of time, the Battle of Armageddon will fill the fields of war with the blood of the enemies of God. The event will be so horrific that the Bible says the blood will flow five feet deep for almost two hundred miles. Revelation 14:20: "And the winepress was trodden without the city, *and blood* came out of the winepress, even unto the horse bridles, by the space of a thousand and six hundred furlongs."

One of the last things Jesus taught us while on this earth was about the *cup*. He was having His last supper with His disciples before His crucifixion. This is what the Lord said (Luke 22:20): "This cup is the new testament *in my blood*, which is shed for you." There is enough blood in that cup to save every man, woman, and child who would call unto Him for forgiveness. It will take the blood of all those who rejected Him to fill the cup of His indignation. This will be the *cup of his wrath*. It will perfectly balance the magnificence of His love and anger, His forgiveness and His judgment.

The church needs to be making this message clear. The desperate condition of the lost should compel us to be about our Father's business. The sermons should be calling us to battle against the evil that surrounds us. 2 Corinthians 10:4: "For the weapons of our warfare are not carnal, but mighty through God to the pulling down of strongholds." It seems, however, that believers would rather design churches to be more like country clubs. We are called to be soldiers of the Lord. Upon salvation, God enlists us into His army that we might bring the gospel into enemy territory. Too much time is being spent on comforting the congregation instead of training the troops.

Our weapon is the Word of God, and our method is love. Real expression of love gives clear warning to the lost. The sharing of the *terror of the Lord* could well be the last message of love offered before the Cup of God's wrath is poured out.

CHAPTER TWELVE

— THE FEAR OF THE LORD —

"The fear of the Lord is a fountain of life, to depart from the snares of death" (Proverbs 14:27).

T his book has dealt with some strong words and seldom-used Scriptures having to do with God's character. We have examined His wrath, His anger, and His fury among others. "The fear of the Lord" is an additional phrase that demands a closer look if we are to expand and balance our understanding of God. The multitude of sermons preached on the love and mercy of God in combination with a scarcity of teaching on His judgment has led us to water down this phrase. If you ask the average church attendee today to define the "fear of the Lord," you are inclined to get some feedback on how we are to reverence God and give Him due respect. While that is undoubtedly true, it is woefully lacking in real depth to the full meaning of the phrase.

It was reported in Acts 9:31, the church was continually *"walking in the fear of the Lord."* Paul wrote to the Philippian church to "work out their salvation in *fear and trembling."* The concept of fear and trembling is not a widespread view in today's understanding of the nature of God. Bear in mind, however, that these are New Testament verses. This is how the early church interpreted their responsibility in walking with the Lord. There was nothing flippant or shallow in their sensitivity to the Holy Spirit of God. Acts 9:31: "Then had the churches rest throughout all Judaea and Galilee and Samaria and were edified, and *walking in the fear of the Lord*, and in the comfort of the Holy Ghost." Their esteem for God reflected a high regard for the consequences of displeasing Him.

The Lord will instruct us if we will listen. Psalms 34:11: "Come, ye children, hearken unto me: *I will teach you the fear of the Lord*." We must pay close attention to His commands. We must give weight to the significance of His directions on living if we are to understand the fear of the Lord. He is calling us to give Him an unspoiled heart. 2 Chronicles 19:9: "And he charged them, saying, 'Thus shall ye do in the fear of the Lord, faithfully, and *with a perfect heart*.'" Wisdom and knowledge and understanding come when we turn from evil and ask Him to create that new heart within us. Job 28:28: "And unto man he said, *Behold, the fear of the Lord, that is wisdom; and to depart from evil is understanding*." We cannot continually taint our hearts with sin and rightfully believe we are walking in the fear of the Lord.

We must make a choice. It is our concern over God's displeasure that helps us to stay on course. But, there are those that do not choose this wisdom. Proverbs 1:7 "The fear of the Lord is the beginning of knowledge: *but fools despise wisdom and instruction*."

We tend to believe that Christians are not guilty of an unclean heart, yet ask yourself: why is there so much apostasy in the church? Why do only 20 percent of the congregation do 80 percent of the work? Have we forgotten whom it is that we should fear? Matthew 10:28: "And fear not them which kill the body, but are not able to kill the soul: but rather fear him which is able to destroy both soul and body in hell."

Reverence and *awe* are generally accepted definitions of the fear of the Lord, but that does not necessarily imply "trembling." Trembling in the Greek language is the word *tromos*. It denotes a quaking with fear. Christians will go to church when they want to go, and they will not go when they don't want to go. That does not sound much like trembling. We should be troubled to cause an offense to God in any way. The Bible says that we should dread to insult our Savior.

This is a wakeup call to the dull of hearing. There is a right way to live our Christianity. Some will continue to complain and say they don't want to hear about the fires of hell. Dear Christian, your works will be judged by fire. 1 Corinthians 3:13, 15: "Every man's work shall be made manifest: for the day shall declare it because it shall be *revealed by fire*; and the fire shall try every man's work of what sort it is. . . . If any man's work shall be burned, he shall suffer loss: but he himself shall be saved; yet so *as by fire*." According to this passage, it is possible to be saved but not live in the fear of the Lord. What a terrible loss that is, both in this world and in the world to come. The fires of God's judgment are burning. They are ready to be poured upon the chaff of this world. Revelation 20:9: "And fire came down from God out of heaven and devoured them." The world will run and hide from this future event when God pours forth His wrath. Isaiah 2:19, 21: "And they shall go into the holes of the rocks, and into the caves of the earth, for *fear of the Lord*, and for the glory of his majesty, when he ariseth to shake terribly the earth. . . . To go into the clefts of the rocks, and into the tops of the ragged rocks, for *fear of the Lord*, and for the glory of his majesty, when he ariseth to shake terribly the earth."

BLESSINGS

Given the full nature of God, there is good news. He shows His favor in tremendous ways when we take responsibility for our actions and turn to Him for strength and forgiveness. Consider the blessings that come if you do make the choice to live by the fear of the Lord.

1. **It is the beginning of knowledge and wisdom**. Psalms 111:10: "*The fear of the Lord* is the beginning of wisdom." Wisdom is the intelligent use of the knowledge we have.

Knowledge that stems from the fear of the Lord is steeped in virtuous living. Exercising our obedience and faith with the Lord's presence in mind is a worthy duty that leads us to an eternal bliss of uninterrupted joy. It is a fool who forgets the purpose for which he was brought into the world. Woe to the man who overlooks the finality of his existence.

2. **It will turn you from evil.** *Pro 8:13: "The fear of the Lord is to hate evil."* We are born into this world sinners. Our nature is diametrically opposed to the Holiness of God. If we call to Him to change us, he makes us a new creation in Him. What He loves, we should love. What He hates, we should hate. To turn from our wicked ways puts us in alignment with His holiness, whereby we become one with Him.

3. **It will prolong life.** Proverbs 10:27: *"The fear of the Lord prolongeth days: but the years of the wicked shall be shortened."* All things being equal, the Christian life is a healthy life. We do not give in to the excesses of the flesh. We understand the truth that the wages of sin are death. We turn our backs on evil. Unbelievers plow ahead with their natural inclinations, to their death. It is equally true that from the time of Abel's murder to the day when Stephen "fell asleep" there have been those who lived in the fear of the Lord yet died an early death. Something more must be considered in this verse. The believer lives more in a day ("prolongeth days") than the unbeliever does in a year. The Bible says that "God is love." No one really knows love until they have met the God of love. The Christian experiences more love and joy in a year than the lost person can possibly know in a lifetime. Living in the fear of the Lord is not a curse. It is a privileged life because the curse of death has been broken.

4. **It will give you a ready assurance in God.** Proverbs 14:26: "In *the fear of the Lord* is strong confidence: and his children shall have a place of refuge." The old hymn says it best:

"Blessed assurance, Jesus is mine." Living in the fear of the Lord never implies you could lose your salvation. Salvation is given in a moment when we are born again. We become a new creature in Christ Jesus. Nothing can take us from His hand. We are saved from the power of sin, and we are saved from the punishment of hell. If we are saved from those two, then we could never be condemned to them again. The Lord can correct us, He can chastise us, but He will never condemn us (Romans 8:1): "There is therefore *now no condemnation to them which are in Christ Jesus*, who walk not after the flesh, but after the Spirit." The more profound our conviction to walk in the fear of the Lord, the more we will be strengthened in our confidence in knowing that we will always have a place with our God.

5. **It will give you a zest for life.** Proverbs 14:27: "*The fear of the Lord* is a fountain of life, to depart from the snares of death." Life is worth living. We were given life by Almighty God that we might come to Him and live to glorify Him. How sad it is to hear each time the news reports another suicide. According to the American Foundation for Suicide Prevention (AFSP), more than 44,000 people try to commit suicide each year in the United States. In 2015, suicide was the second-leading cause of death in people 15 to 34 years of age and the third-leading cause of death in children *ages 10 to 14*, according to the CDC. Living in the presence of the Lord gives us a real enthusiasm for what comes next. Our passion in life becomes our passion for life. Jesus said, "I am the life." To know Him is to love Him. To love Him is to live for Him. John 10:10: "The thief cometh not, but for to steal, and to kill, and to destroy: *I am come that they might have life, and that they might have it more abundantly*."

6. **It is the key to living a satisfied life.** Proverbs 19:23: "*The fear of the Lord* tendeth to life: and he that hath it shall abide

satisfied; he shall not be visited with evil." The Christian is not immune from trouble, but we have the hope of His protection and the grace that will be sufficient enough for anything that comes our way. The wicked lives without the fear of the Lord. He lives to fulfill the lusts of the flesh, he acts according to his own will, he speaks blasphemies, and he meditates on evil day and night, as if there were no God witnessing and taking heed to his every thought and word and deed. *No one can be satisfied with anything until he or she can be satisfied that God is the only thing.* To the hymn writer, we say "Amen": "I'd rather have Jesus than anything this world affords today."

7. **It will provide your needs and desires in life.** Proverbs 22:4: "By humility and *the fear of the Lord* are riches, and honour, and life." Humility is an added requirement to the fear of the Lord if we are to receive the promise of riches and honour in this life. Humility is the good habit of a spiritual walk. It is apparent not only in how we treat people we consider our equals but is likewise perceivable in the way we handle our relationships with those who are our superiors and those we deem inferior. Humility treats all men with respect and love. *Humility determines that it is alright that we be last that others might be first.* We must so reverence God's splendor and power that we willingly submit to the commands of his Word. This means there is a godly contentment with the way He chooses to bless us. We are never to get caught up in comparing our lives with the lives of others. Proverbs 23:17: "Let not thine heart envy sinners: but be thou in *the fear of the Lord* all the day long." We must behave humbly toward God and man. Where the fear of the Lord is there will be humility.

A humble person accepts what the Lord says and tries to live by His precepts. Living with a perfect heart is accomplished with a keen belief in His ability to create a new spirit within us. God is not concerned with our stature and prominence in this world, but He offers wonderful blessings to those who will walk humbly with Him. 2 Chronicles 19:7, 9: "Wherefore now let *the fear of the Lord* be upon you; take heed and do it: for there is no iniquity with the Lord our God, nor respect of persons, nor taking of gifts. . . . And he charged them, saying, 'Thus shall ye do in *the fear of the Lord*, faithfully, and with *a perfect heart.*'"

TAKE HEED

The Lord sends preachers into this world to warn of the consequences of living a life apart from Him. He sends judges into the world to strike terror into the hearts of evildoers in the hope of their repentance. Someday soon the angels of Heaven will be sent to execute judgment upon those who would not listen. For those who will not take heed, the words of Job express the *terror of the Lord* (Job 31:23): "For destruction from *God was a terror to me*, and by reason of his highness I could not endure." For those who will take heed and live in the fear of the Lord, God promises that His terror is not for them (Job 33:7): "Behold, *my terror shall not make thee afraid*, neither shall my hand be heavy upon thee."

Without the fear of the Lord we put a tremendous distance between ourselves and the gifts of God's abundant wisdom. If we ignore this element of His nature, we can be tempted to flirt with evil and all its destructive power. We will not know the depth of God's love for us, and the assurance of our salvation will be shaken. Without this fear, we will not be motivated to repent. Without this awe of Him, we will not work out our salvation in "fear and trembling."

There is eternal mercy for those that fear God and understand the importance of keeping His commandments. Psalms 103:17, 18: "But the mercy of the Lord is from everlasting to everlasting upon them *that fear him*; To such as *keep his covenant*, and to those that *remember his commandments to do them.*"

We should not take either His justice or His love to an extreme. Both these attributes are in perfect harmony within His character. Each of these qualities must hold equal sway in our perception of Him if we are to truly understand the nature of our God. This balance is developed by a consistent study of the Word of God. In the book of Deuteronomy (31:12), Moses commanded that every seven years the Scriptures were to be read to "*everyone that they may hear, and that they may learn, and fear the Lord your God, and observe to do all the words of this law.*" The writer of Hebrews put it this way (4:1): "*Let us, therefore, fear, lest, a promise being left us of entering into his rest, any of you should seem to come short of it.*" We certainly do not want to come up short of anything the Lord has for us. Every good and perfect gift comes from Him. Let us work diligently to enter into this rest that the Scriptures promise us, and to continue to remain there.

We should read the whole Word of God. We should not pick and choose only those parts we like. It we follow the whole council of God we will keep in balance the fullness of all His traits and will protect against taking anything about Him to an extreme.

*"Though a sinner do evil an hundred times, and his days be prolonged, yet surely, I know that **it shall be well with them that fear God**, which fear before him" (Ecclesiastes 8:12).*

Chapter Thirteen

—————— Judgment ——————

*"He is the Rock, his work is perfect: for **all his ways are judgment**: a God of truth and without iniquity, just and right is he" (Deuteronomy 32:4).*

Twenty-eight hundred years ago, God called a certain preacher to deliver a final message to a city full of sinners. The preacher's name was Jonah. The city was called Nineveh. The sermon was short and to the point. "Yet forty days, and Nineveh shall be overthrown" (Jonah 3:4). It may have been the shortest sermon ever preached. There was no offer of salvation. There was no three-point sermon outline on how to be reconciled to God. There were no illustrations of God's mercy or His grace. It was a formidable message on judgment to come. It took Jonah three days to walk across the vast city of Nineveh. He continually repeated this gripping announcement of doom. Those eight words resounded with increased intensity as they echoed up the alleys and down the streets to all one hundred and twenty thousand citizens of that great city. Judgment was coming, and it was coming soon. They had forty days left to live.

Then something miraculous happened. The entire town believed God and repented (Jonah 3:5): "So the people of *Nineveh believed*

God, and proclaimed a fast, and put on sackcloth, *from the greatest of them even to the least of them.*" Grasp, for a moment, what transpired. A backslidden messenger of God delivers the shortest sermon ever preached to some of the vilest people who have ever lived—and all were saved. More souls gave their heart to the Lord during those days than from any other message in recorded history. Do not miss the critical point. The message was a warning of *judgment.*

There is an important principle that we should learn from this story of Jonah. When God warns of judgment, there is an implied offer of forgiveness. Even though Jonah did not mention an alternative to God's judgment, the Lord held the option open for forgiveness. When Nineveh repented, it was then that the Lord showed mercy— and His judgment was postponed. History tells us that it was another one hundred years before God destroyed the city. In the days of Noah, He waited one hundred and twenty years from the time of His warning until the flood came. Even the cities of Sodom and Gomorrah could have been spared had there been ten righteous souls found. If mercy were not extended there would be no need for the warning of judgment to come. God is not obligated to tell us ahead of time when He will judge us. But He chooses to communicate His displeasure and the impending consequences in the hope that we will listen and repent and turn back to Him.

There seems to be a cut-rate brand of Christianity in circulation today. Anytime judgment is preached it is summarily dismissed as out of touch with the present-day understanding of God. Today's religious expression rejects any notion of judgment to come. It seems that the prevailing attitude of the church toward any mention of judgment is that it is old-fashioned and out of date. People see the description of God using the sword of His wrath to punish sinners as an antiquated view of who He is and how He acts. Let us go back to the Bible again. Job 19:29: *"Be ye afraid* of the sword: for wrath bringeth the punishments of the sword, *that ye may know there is a judgment."* In other words, pay attention to the *terror of the Lord!* The church of this generation relegates God's punishments to being just "Old Testament theology." It is comfortable in its belief that His judgment is in the past and His throne is now a throne of love and mercy. But we cannot ignore the clear words of Scripture. Psalms 9:7: "But the Lord shall endure forever: *he hath prepared his throne for judgment.*" Our Lord is certainly a God of love and mercy, but He is equally full of justice and judgment. Psalms 89:14: *"Justice and judgment* are the habitation of thy *throne: mercy and truth* shall go before thy face."

Men and women of the church today need to open their eyes to the perilous times in which we are living and pay a much deeper regard to God's hatred of all evil in this world. His judgment is faithful and righteous. His judgment is a good thing and not an evil thing. Job 34:12: "Yea, surely *God will not do wickedly, neither will the Almighty pervert judgment.*" His judgment is coming, and the ungodly had better beware. Psalms 1:5, 6: "Therefore the ungodly shall not stand in the *judgment,* but the way of *the ungodly shall perish.*"

Jesus had something remarkable to say about Nineveh (Luke 11:32): "The men of Nineveh shall rise up in the *judgment* with this generation, and shall condemn it: for they repented at the preaching of Jonas; and, behold, a greater than Jonas is here.'" Jesus came that we might have life and have it more abundantly. But we must *choose life.* God is for His saints, but He is against the wicked. Psalms 37:28: "For *the Lord loveth judgment,* and forsaketh not his saints; they are preserved for ever: *but the seed of the wicked shall be cut off.*" How does someone move from sinner to saint? Psalms 37:27: "Depart from evil, and do good, and dwell for evermore." Jesus made a way when there seemed to be no way. Whoever would come to Him would not perish but have everlasting life. This writer is not trying to say you can somehow "earn" your way into Heaven. By the same token, no one can go on in sin as a lifestyle and ever expect to walk through those pearly gates to glory. Nineveh will judge this generation because Nineveh repented and this generation has not.

The Lord's words are captivating. He said the men of Nineveh would rise in *"the judgment."* That means there is a final judgment coming. It must come to settle all the scores of history. All of Nineveh repented. It takes the same repentance today that it took twenty-eight hundred years ago to avoid the judgment of God. Rest assured, however, the judgment will come.

The prophet Daniel was witness to the moment the judgment was to start. Picture this incredible scene he describes (Daniel 7:9, 10): "I beheld till the thrones were cast down, and the Ancient of Days did sit, whose garment was white as snow, and the hair of his head like the pure wool: his throne was like the fiery flame, and his wheels as burning fire. A fiery stream issued and came forth from before him: thousand thousands ministered unto him, and ten thousand times ten thousand stood before him: *the judgment was set*, and the books were opened."

What a dreadful day is coming. The prophet Isaiah saw it coming as well and described it this way (30:27): "Behold, the name of the Lord cometh from far, burning with his anger, and the burden thereof is heavy: his lips are *full of indignation*, and his tongue as a devouring fire."

Indignation is not a word we use much anymore. *Strong's Concordance* helps us understand the depth of its meaning: *zah'-am* — from H2194; strictly "froth at the mouth," that is, (figuratively) fury, especially of God's displeasure with sin: angry, indignation, rage. We can develop a sentence using these words: The Lord's indignation is a holy frothing at the mouth with angry fury and rage rising up from God's displeasure of sin. The writer of the book of Hebrews understood the full ramifications of God's indignation and the coming judgment (10:31): *"It is a fearful thing to fall into the hands of the living God."*

ANOTHER DREAM

Allow me to share a dream I had of the beginning of the Day of The Lord. As the dream opened, I was standing high upon a mountain overlooking the plains of the earth. I could see for miles. It was a beautiful sunny day. The only cloud in the sky stretched low across the entire horizon. I noticed the cloud starting to roll in place like a scroll. While it continued to spin it slowly raised itself up from its horizontal position to a vertical position. The cloud reached from the earth to the apex of the heavens above my head.

Next, it began rolling out to cover the sky and turned from its original white color to a menacing dark billowing cloud. While the cloud swelled in size it took on the shape of a being that I interpreted to be God. It was more threatening than a giant tornado might be. I could not take my eyes off the cloud, but I could see in my peripheral vision that the men of the earth were running for their lives in fear. Everyone was trying to find a place to hide. Not taking my eyes off the cloud, I began to cry out to the men of the earth that they need not be afraid. I called out as loud as I could that all they needed to do was to turn to Him and not run from Him. As I shouted my pleas, I could not bring myself to look away from the cloud. I anticipated that the rapture was about to happen, and I did not want to miss it. It was at that point I awoke from the dream.

The Bible tells of a time, coming in the future, when an event similar to this dream will come to pass. Revelation 6:14-17: "And the heaven departed as *a scroll* when it is *rolled together*, and every mountain and island were moved out of their places. And the kings of the earth, and the great men, and the rich men, and the chief captains, and the mighty men, and every bondman, and every free man, *hid themselves* in the dens and in the rocks of the mountains; And said to the mountains and rocks, Fall on us, and *hide us* from the face of him that sitteth on the throne, and *from the wrath of the Lamb: For the great day of his wrath is come*; and who shall be able to stand?

God's judgment has been exhibited multiple times and in many ways in the past. There have been judgments on individuals such as Adam and Eve being expelled from the Garden and the banishment of Cain for his murder of Abel. There have been citywide judgments like Jericho and Sodom and Gomorrah. God has destroyed great empires.

The Babylonian, Grecian, Persian, and Roman kingdoms have disintegrated to dust under the power of God's hand. Entire armies have been destroyed in a moment by the Lord. Pharaoh's army was drowned when chasing the Hebrews through the Red Sea. The Bible tells the story of 185,000 troops being destroyed in one night! Isaiah 37:36: "Then the angel of the Lord went forth, and smote in the camp of the Assyrians a hundred and fourscore and five thousand: and when they arose early in the morning, behold, they were all dead corpses."

The Lord has systematically dismantled nations for their rejection of Him. Egypt is a prime example. That nation experienced disaster under God's ten-point plan of plagues. And, of course, God judged His chosen race when they worshipped the image of the golden calf. They were left to wander in the wilderness forty years on their way to the Promised Land. Judgment is a very present aspect of the many characteristics of God.

The judgment of Christ on the cross was God's judgment on sin. For all who will believe in what the Lord did on the cross by taking our sins on Him, there will be no more judgment for our iniquities. He died for the sins of the whole world. John 1:29: "The next day John seeth Jesus coming unto him, and saith, *Behold the Lamb of God, which taketh away the sin of the world.*"

Mankind wants judgment. They just don't want judgment to fall on themselves individually. We can see the wretchedness in others. Even lost men want justice in the most horrendous of cases. We are shocked by crimes we deem repulsive. Even though we demand justice be brought to bear in the appalling actions of murderers, child abusers, rapists, and more, our judgments are imperfect. Imagine how fearful it would be if we were to fall under the far more rigid scale of God's judgment for all the things He considers unholy. His scale is perfectly balanced between His judgment and His mercy. The center point of that scale hangs on the cross of Jesus Christ.

There are more judgments to come. The believers will appear at what is commonly referred to as the "judgment seat of Christ." Only believers in the Lord attend this event. 2 Corinthians 5:10: "For we must all appear before *the judgment seat of Christ*; that every one may receive the things done in his body, according to that he hath done, whether it be good or bad." The determination of what is good and what is bad is simple. All things done in love will be rewarded. Anything done without love will be burned as the wood, hay, and stubble. This judgment is not a judgment on our sin. It is not a judgment to see if we make Heaven or not. This is a judgment to determine the rewards given by God for our service to Him while we were on the earth. 1 Corinthians 3:12-15: "Now if any man build upon this foundation gold, silver, precious stones, wood, hay, stubble; Every man's work shall be made manifest: for the day shall declare it, because it shall be revealed by fire; and the fire shall try every man's work of what sort it is. If any man's work abide which he hath built thereupon, he shall receive a reward. If any man's work shall be burned, he shall suffer loss: but he himself shall be saved; yet so as by fire."

God has judged individual nations in the past, but He will rule all nations in the future. While the church in Heaven exits the judgment seat of Christ to attend the marriage supper of the Lamb, the countries of the world will be called to the supper of the great God. This judgment will take place at the time of the end. It will be a grotesque scene of carnage. Revelation 19:17, 18: "And I saw an angel standing in the sun; and he cried with a loud voice, saying *to all the fowls that fly* in the midst of heaven, Come and gather yourselves together unto *the supper of the great God*; That ye may eat the flesh of kings, and the flesh of captains, and the flesh of mighty men, and the flesh of horses, and of them that sit on them, and the flesh of all men, both free and bond, both small and great." Falling under the judgment of god will be a violent end. There was nothing appealing about the blood on the cross of Jesus Christ. Sin is as ugly as it gets. The judgment on sin was a horrifying spectacle when Jesus was crucified. It will be equally gruesome when the hardheartedness of men is dealt its final blow. Romans 2:5: "But after thy hardness and impenitent heart treasurest up unto thyself wrath against the day of wrath and revelation of the righteous judgment of God."

There is good news. God has made a way of escape. We can judge ourselves. If our assessment of ourselves lines up with God's Word and we repent, we will not be judged. We can accept what Jesus did for us. We can appropriate His death, and the Lord will spare us. 1 Corinthians 11:31: "For if we would *judge ourselves, we should not be judged.*" There is no better offer than this. There will never be a better offer than this. We must be completely honest before Him. He will know the difference. 2 Peter 2:9: "The Lord knoweth how to deliver the godly out of temptations and to reserve the unjust unto the day of judgment to be punished."

The Lord has not only judged individuals and armies, nations and empires; He has judged angels. He also judged the entire world with the flood of Noah. If He spared not any of these, neither will He spare anyone who rejects His Son and what Jesus was willing to do to keep us from the judgment of God. 2 Peter 2:4-7: "For if God *spared not the angels that sinned,* but cast them down to hell, and delivered them into chains of darkness, to be reserved unto judgment; And *spared not the old world,* but saved Noah the eighth person, a preacher of righteousness, bringing in the flood upon the world of the ungodly; And *turning the cities of Sodom and Gomorrah into ashes* condemned them with an overthrow, making them an ensample unto those that after should live ungodly . . . " Let us stop there and ask: "Shouldn't we call upon the Lord before it is too late?"

*"Fear God, and give glory to him; for **the hour of his judgment is come:** and worship him that made heaven, and earth, and the sea, and the fountains of waters (Revelation 14:7)."*

Chapter Fourteen

——— The Love of God ———

*"In this was manifested the **love of God** toward us,
because that God sent his only begotten Son into the
world, that we might live through him"* (1 John 4:9).

G od is love! That is what the Bible says. His love is not one of His
attributes, but love is His very essence. God loved the world so
much that He gave His Son Jesus that whoever would believe in Him
would not perish in the judgment to come but be given the gift of
eternal life. His offer of love was, and is, to anyone and everyone who
would choose to believe in Him. It has been that way for generations:
whoever would come, could come.

There are those who understand how deep the love of God must
go to be willing to ask His Son to suffer crucifixion to pay for our sins.
Believers should have no fear of the judgment to come. 1 John 4:16,
17: "And we have known and believed the love that God hath to us.
God is love, and he that dwelleth in love dwelleth in God, and God
in him. Herein is our love made perfect, *that we may have boldness in
the day of judgment*."

The Father in Heaven is omnibenevolent. In other words, He is
all good all the time. God does not need to "turn off" His anger to "turn

on" His love. Neither does He need to "turn off" His love to "turn on" His anger. Both His anger and love exist in Him at all times. Both of these were on display and equally demonstrated on the day Jesus was crucified. God never changes. Malachi 3:6: "For I am the Lord, *I change not.*"

God, who is love, wanted to express that love and receive love in return. So in the beginning the triune Godhead created the setting whereby He could do just that. He made Adam and Eve in His image and gave them the freedom to choose. The Lord was just and fair in telling them that there were blessings if they chose to love and obey Him and there were consequences if they chose to disobey Him. They could eat of everything in the garden except for the fruit of *one tree.* Of course, we know that they chose wrongly. The aftermath of that decision brought death to them and, thereby, death to all mankind. It was not the fruit that brought their death; it was their disobedience to God.

The Scriptures give us insight into the depth of God's love on this point. The rebellion of Adam and Eve did not catch the Lord off guard. The plan to correct their disobedience was laid before the first day of creation. Hebrews 4:3: "For we which have believed do enter into rest, as he said, As I have *sworn in my wrath* if they shall enter into my rest: although *the works were finished from the foundation of the world.*"

When Adam and Eve defied the Lord and chose to ignore His warning, it stirred His wrath. It was precisely at this time that He swore we had a way back into His rest if we would believe Him. Love already had a plan for our salvation. Jesus was coming. He was coming to save us. It was the love of God and all His kindness toward us that cared enough to deliver us from the penalty of bad choices and show us mercy. Titus 3:4, 5: "But after that, the kindness and *love of God our Saviour toward man appeared,* Not by works of righteousness which we have done, *but according to his mercy he saved us.*" It was love that motivated God to save us. It was love that motivated Christ to die for us. It is love that motivates us to live for Christ. First Corinthians chapter thirteen reveals some of the depth to which God's love is demonstrated.

Love:
1. **Suffers long:** Consider how patient He has been with men down through the ages and just how longsuffering to each of us individually.

   Remember how much Jesus suffered to bring us salvation.
2. **Is kind:** Jesus said: "Learn of me for I am meek and lowly." There has never been a kinder person to walk this earth. He fed people. He healed people. He raised people from the dead. He loved people.
3. **Bears all things:** Jesus bore our iniquities and bears our burdens. His blood covers our failings, and He carries us until we can walk again.
4. **Believes all things:** No matter how many times we may fall, the Lord believes we will make the right choice next time to let Him live through us.
5. **Endures all things:** The cross proved that. We will never understand all that Jesus went through the day He was crucified. He did not deserve that treatment. He was perfect.

Love is the greatest of all commandments. Jesus said (Matthew 22:37): "Thou shalt love the Lord thy God with all thy heart, and with all thy soul, and with all thy mind. This is the first and great commandment. And the second is like, unto it, Thou shalt love thy neighbour as thyself." This kind of love lets the believer know that he is saved. 1 John 3:14: "*We know that we have passed from death unto life because we love* the brethren." This type of love can be extended even to our enemies. As was stated earlier: God is love, and all love comes from Him.

1 John 4:7: "Beloved, let us love one another: for *love is of God, and every one that loveth is born of God, and knoweth God.*" Without the presence of this manner of love, there is no redemption.

This book has focused on the *terror of the Lord*. Paul told the Corinthian church in his second letter that our knowledge of that terror was good reason to persuade men to consider the condition of their lost souls before God. In Paul's first letter to that same church, he extolled the great love that exemplifies God. The sharing of His love and His terror should be kept in balance. It can be difficult for a pastor to keep the scales level in one sermon (or for that matter, in one book), but over time, the messages should keep the pendulum centered. Most certainly, the overall communication of the character of God presented by the church to the world should offer this well-balanced understanding of God's nature.

It is sad to watch what men and women will spend their time doing while ignoring the love of God. They spend their energies in pursuit of meaningless treasures while forgetting what is promised to come. The Lord seems utterly irrelevant to them while the things that are of no importance consume their every thought and effort. If God had not told us of all the blessings to come to those who believe or had He forgotten to warn of all the curses that await those who have turned a deaf ear to Him, we might have had an excuse for our actions. But it is sealed in His Word, and Christians profess to believe it.

What a great love the Lord has for us! He knew us before we were born and chose a plan for our lives before creation. He is familiar with everything about us. His knowledge is so intricate that He has the very hairs of our head numbered. He desires to lavish His love on us precisely because He is a God of love. We are fearfully and wonderfully made, and He knitted us together while we were in our mother's womb. Every good gift that we receive in this life comes from Him. He is the provider of all our needs, and He will never cease doing good to us.

You may ask yourself, "Why?" It is because He sees us as His treasured possession. He wants us to call Him Father, and He sees us as His children. His thoughts toward each of us are as countless as the grains of sand on a seashore. He has a plan to show us great and mighty things we cannot even imagine. He wants to give us the desires of our heart, and He is able to give to us abundantly more than we could ask or think. The Lord heals our broken hearts and will one day take away all our pain and suffering. Jesus shed Himself of His majesty and gave up everything He had in His Father's kingdom that He might gain our love.

We have been invited to the marriage supper of the Lamb. It will be the greatest celebration this universe has ever seen. He loves us with an everlasting love. He is waiting just a little longer for those who may still choose to be reconciled to Himself. His longsuffering is evidence that He is for us and not against us. How shall we respond? How much longer will He wait?

Solomon, the wisest man who ever lived, gives an excellent summation and perfect counsel to consider.

> *"Let us hear the conclusion of the whole matter: Fear God, and keep his commandments: for this is the whole duty of man. For God shall bring every work into judgment, with every secret thing, whether it be good, or whether it be evil"* (Ecclesiastes 12:13, 14).

— The Plan of Salvation —

*"When once the master of the house is risen up, and
hath shut to the door, and ye begin to stand without,
and to knock at the door, saying, 'Lord, Lord, open
unto us'; and he shall answer and say unto you,
'I know you not whence ye are'" (Luke 13:25).*

This book is a warning of the dangers of rejecting God. It has
shown the devices Satan uses to tempt and deceive humanity.
This manuscript has described the horrors of hell and made it clear
that hell is the result of refusing God's offer of forgiveness. These pages
have described the Lord's characteristics of anger and fury toward the
wickedness of rebellion against Him. This book has endeavored to
describe what just a cup of God's wrath will bring those who decline
His call to be reconciled to Himself.

The crucifixion has been explained. Jesus Christ, the Son of
God, paid the price for our sins. To snub this sacrificial act of God's
love is to forget the *fear of the Lord*. The *terror of the Lord* is a plea to
kiss the Son, with the kiss of adoration and thanksgiving, lest He be

angry and His wrath is kindled "but a little." This book is a cry to all who read it to consider your soul and avoid the judgment to come.

When Adam and Eve rebelled, man was separated from God through sin. God's holiness required punishment for sin, and this punishment was eternal death. Our death is not adequate to cover the penalty for our sin. Only a perfect sacrifice, offered in just the right way, can pay the required price for our sin. Jesus, the perfect God-man, came to offer us redemption and forgiveness. Jesus' death is considered ample payment by God for the sins of the whole world. God loves us and desires an intimate relationship with us. The Bible is the unfolding plan of salvation the Lord has provided for us.

What You Must Do to Be Saved

1. **Admit you are a sinner.** Not *your* definition of a sinner, but accepting the Bible's definition of a sinner.
2. **Recognize there is nothing you can do to save yourself.** Salvation is not your effort to do better or turn over a new leaf. It is not what you can do, but what God has already done.
3. **Believe in what the Lord has done for you to pay for your sins.** God required penalty for sin. Jesus paid the perfect price.
4. **Believe that what He did is sufficient.** There is nothing you can add to secure your salvation.
5. **Personally call on Him for mercy and forgiveness.** The destination of your soul is your responsibility.
6. **Pray to Him using your own words.** Let your prayer come from a humble and sorrowful heart.
7. **Believe He has heard you and answered your prayer for salvation.** His Holy Spirit will reside in you from that time forward and you will be assured of the eternal life He has promised.

8. **Read the Bible daily.** Memorize verses as they speak to you.
9. **Live the rest of your life to glorify Him.** Be motivated by your love for who He is and what He has done for you.

> *"These things have I written unto you that believe on the name of the Son of God; that ye may know that ye have eternal life, and that ye may believe on the name of the Son of God" (1 John 5:13).*